The Branch Librarians' Handbook

The Branch Librarians' Handbook

Vickie Rivers

McFarland & Company, Inc., Publishers
Jefferson, North Carolina, and London

Acknowledgments

Intellectual Freedom Manual, 6th ed. (paper) by the Office for Intellectual Freedom (OIF). Copyright 2004 by the American Library Association. Reproduced with permission of the American Library Association in the format Other Book via the Copyright Clearance Center. *Sexual Harassment Manual for Managers and Supervisors: How to Prevent and Resolve Sexual Harassment Complaints in the Workplace* by Paul Gibson. Copyright 2004 by CCH. Reproduced with permission of CCH in the format Other Book via Copyright Clearance Center. *Whole Library Handbook 2: Current Data, Professional Advice, and Curiosa about Libraries and Library Services* by George M. Eberhart. Copyright 2004 by the American Library Association. Reproduced with permission of the American Library Association in the format Other Book via Copyright Clearance Center. *Whole Library Handbook 3: Current Data, Professional Advice, and Curiosa about Libraries and Library Service* (paper) by George M. Eberhart. Copyright 2004 by the American Library Association. Reproduced with permission of the American Library Association in the format Other Book via Copyright Clearance Center.
Dallas Public Library mission statement reproduced by permission of Dallas Public Library. Dayton Metro Library mission statement reproduced by permission of Dayton Metro Library. "Supervising Library Professionals" by Darlene Severance reproduced by permission of Darlene Severance.

LIBRARY OF CONGRESS CATALOGUING-IN-PUBLICATION DATA

Rivers, Vickie, 1956–
The branch librarians' handbook / Vickie Rivers.
p.   cm.
Includes bibliographical references and index.

ISBN 0-7864-1821-4 (softcover : 50# alkaline paper) ∞

1. Branch libraries—Administration—Handbooks, manuals, etc.
2. Public libraries—Administration—Handbooks, manuals, etc.
I. Title.
Z686.R58   2004   025.1'974—dc22   2004015873

British Library cataloguing data are available

Cover photograph ©2004 PhotoDisc

Manufactured in the United States of America

McFarland & Company, Inc., Publishers
Box 611, Jefferson, North Carolina 28640
www.mcfarlandpub.com

To my children, Robin and Brandon,
who give me joy and their unconditional love

Table of Contents

Introduction

Libraries are integral parts of our communities. Users have visited libraries in record numbers over recent years. We as librarians must be able to meet the needs of our current users and be able to recruit new users. Libraries today have thousands of books, audiovisual materials, framed prints, and computers. Services vary from library to library; one library may offer patrons the chance to check out only a few books, while another may offer unlimited checkout of all kinds of materials. Users may have access to the Internet, adult and children's programming, classes in English as a second language, and meeting-room facilities. Libraries serve people of all races, religions, socioeconomic groups, and ages. Every user who visits our libraries wants and deserves equal access and treatment. Librarians need training in how to effectively serve their users and manage their branches.

Managing a branch library will be one of the most exciting challenges of your professional career. I have worked at main and branch libraries and there are distinct differences between them. Main libraries are usually the largest in the library system and employ the largest staff. They may be located near the center of town and be surrounded by other businesses. Their collections are large and general in nature. Their circulation statistics may be the highest in the library system because of the high numbers of patrons.

Branch libraries are located near residential communities. They are neighborhood libraries used by patrons in or near the area where the branches are located. Patrons love the opportunity to visit and to be served by their branch library. Many patrons for one reason or another will never visit the main library. They have commented to me that the main library is too far away or too large, that parking is a problem, or that they just like the atmosphere of a branch library better. At branch libraries patrons get to know the staff and we as librarians get to know our regular patrons. Depending upon the size of your branch, your staff may be able to spend more time with each patron and give them more personal service than they could receive at a busy main library.

The collections of branch libraries should reflect the needs of the community they serve. For example, if there is a large population of Hispanic people in the community, branch managers should order materials to meet the needs of their Spanish-speaking patrons. Branch managers need to be able to evaluate their communities and make sure that their collections are adequate for all patrons served.

Branch library managers need to be trained to handle all of the duties involved in running their branches effectively. They need to be able to make decisions that are the best for the branch and to do this in a timely manner. When a situation arises, you may not have time to call someone for guidance. You need to know things like what to do when the police have to be called, how to handle patron and staff emergencies, and what to do if the copier breaks down. Everything that goes on in your branch is essentially your responsibility.

This book is designed to answer your questions about branch management and to offer encouragement. It will also give you commonsense approaches to managing your branch. I hope that you will take some of these suggestions and apply them to your position. You will find that your job will be much easier, more enjoyable, and very rewarding.

This book is meant to give managers a single source for help in dealing with issues that almost certainly will arise. When I became a branch manager for the first time, I didn't know what to expect. I searched for a book that would include the many duties of a branch manager. All I found were individual titles on various library-related issues. They didn't seem like practical guides, and I did not have time to read multiple books while learning a new job. For many years I learned while on the job, attended workshops, talked to other branch managers, and read what books I could.

After years of management experience I decided to write this book to help new managers settle into their positions. In addition, this book is also for existing managers who want to further develop their skills and enhance their knowledge. No matter the size of your library, you can apply these techniques immediately. Be sure to take your time and set realistic goals for yourself in order to become the best manager possible.

1

The Mission Statement

A mission statement is the written documentation stating your library system's purpose and the reason for its existence. Mission statements include things that your library is already doing, what the goals of the library are, and how those goals will be achieved. It may be one sentence, one paragraph, or a page long. Read the mission statement for your library system. If there isn't one, locate one from another library system to see what it looks like. Read the mission statement for your branch. If there isn't one, create one that will communicate your goals. Get input from your staff.

Your mission statement should be direct and very professional. Include quality of service to your patrons and specific aspects of your library's programs and services. Think about your collection-development goals and how they pertain to your users. Include such things as community involvement, marketing plans, technological accessibility, public trust, facilities maintenance, staff services, and inclusiveness of your users. Read your mission statement often. Make sure that your entire staff reads and understands it. Fulfill the mission of your branch.

The following are two examples of well-written mission statements, from the Dallas Public Library in Texas, and the Dayton Metro Library in Ohio.

Dallas Public Library's Mission Statement

> The Mission of the Dallas Public Library is to link resources and customers to enhance lives. The Library is committed to inform, entertain, enrich, and to foster the self-learning process by facilitating access to its collections, services, and facilities to all members of the community. All service efforts will focus on customer expectations and needs.
>
> The Library will make available a broad spectrum of ideas reflecting diverse points of view and will provide collections that reflect the need and diversity of the community it serves.
>
> The Library will honor its public trust by assuring maximum use of public resources. Furthermore, the Library will stimulate the

awareness and use of libraries to promote individual enlightenment, community enrichment, and economic vitality throughout the city.

[Reprinted with permission.]

Dayton Metro Library's Mission Statement

The mission of the Dayton Metro Library is to respond to the interests and needs of its community by providing recorded information and thought.

Goals

1. Continue as the most comprehensive source of information for the community.

2. Strengthen and provide community resources through cooperation with other libraries and community agencies.

3. Ensure that the library is user oriented and meets the needs of all who require special assistance.

4. Actively promote our programs, materials, services and role in fostering free communication within our democratic society.

5. Structure our organization and manage our operations effectively.

6. Preserve our rare and valuable materials for continuing use.

7. Provide special programs to encourage use of the library.

8. Provide training and development opportunities to library staff for occupational and professional growth.

9. Provide a collection of materials and technological tools that accesses information that meets the interests and needs of the community and represents various points of view on controversial subjects.

10. Develop sources of funding to supplement the Library and Local Government Support Fund.

11. Monitor and respond to trends and developments in library practices.

12. Provide assistance and training to the public through knowledgeable and customer oriented Staff.

Strategies

• Continue the Total Quality Management philosophy and attitude throughout the library.

• Employ appropriate technologies.

• Emphasize staff development and training.

- Increase the awareness of the library's role and its importance to its community.

- Provide physical facilities to meet the challenges of the 21st century.

- Develop and maintain sources of supplemental funding.

- Assist and train our customers in the use of new technology available at the library.

- Strengthen governmental relations.

[Adopted May 21, 1997, by the Board of Trustees of the Dayton Metro Library, Dayton, Ohio. Reprinted with permission.]

2

The Library System

The main library, all of the branches, and the bookmobile make up the typical library system. Ask for a copy of the history of your library system and research local newspapers and in-house printed sources. Talk to staff who have worked for the library system for many years to find out how the library system began and how it has evolved over the years. This should give you some insight into where it might be headed. Also, look at the history of your branch. Find out what the circulation statistics were five years ago and what they are now. Is usage of your branch growing or remaining the same? What about programming? Is the attendance at programs increasing, decreasing, or remaining the same? Know what the roles are for each branch in the system. It will help you understand why their collections are different. Make sure your branch is actively fulfilling its role in the community.

Goals and Objectives

Read the goals and objectives for your library system. Goals are plans that you would like to achieve and objectives are specific ways in which you plan to achieve those goals. See what specific goals were developed for each branch. The goals should be very specific with attainable results. Each goal should have a date by which it will be achieved.

In addition to understanding the goals of your library system, read the goals and objectives for your branch. If there aren't any or if you can't locate them, develop your own. At the end of each year, review how many goals you have met. Set goals and objectives for yourself, your branch, and your staff. When setting your goals, include all aspects of library service. Include such things as ways to increase circulation, new programming, collection development, and any projects that you would like to do. Be specific in your goals; don't use vague generalizations.

Don't set unachievable goals such as registering every person in your community for a library card. There will always be people who will never visit the library. A more appropriate goal would be to increase the number of people in the community with library cards by 5 percent. An objective for that goal would be to visit all schools in the community and register every child for a library card. Knowing about the library system as a whole will help you to better understand how your branch fits into the system and what direction it should take to serve its users and achieve the library system's goals.

Departments in the Library System

You may or may not have all of the following departments in your library system. Some are only on the system level; others are also found in the branches. It is helpful to know the purpose of other departments in the library system. It will help you to know whom to contact when you have questions or problems in these areas. The following are some of the departments you can expect to find in a medium- to large-sized library system.

Acquisitions

The Acquisitions Department is a part of or works closely with the Collection Development Department. It places orders for items to be cataloged and added to the various library collections. Centralized ordering occurs when the Collection Development Department selects and places orders for materials for the entire library system. Either department may approve invoices for payment. It may also communicate with vendors and publishers about ordering specific materials.

Administration

The library system's administration includes the director, deputy director, and others who work in that department. The director is the manager of the entire library system. The deputy director acts as the director in the absence of the director and assists in those necessary duties.

Bookmobile

If your library system is large enough to have a bookmobile, make sure that all staff know where the current schedule is, what the procedures are for handling bookmobile items, and what fees are charged. Some bookmobiles charge per missed stop, not per day. You don't want to overcharge a patron. Don't refer all calls concerning the bookmobile to the Extension department. Ask the bookmobile staff what their policies are so that your staff can answer patron questions. Many times the bookmobile is on the road and patrons calling will not be able to speak to anyone directly. Ask the manager of the bookmobile department if you can go with them to some of their stops. Being on the bookmobile and knowing their procedures will help you to explain these procedures to your staff and patrons.

Collection Development

The Collection Development Department is responsible for developing policies and establishing criteria for the selection of materials. It disseminates information to the entire system on weeding, inclusion of patron donations, reconsideration of materials, and any issues pertaining to the library's collection. The Collection Development Department analyzes the communities served by each branch and makes ordering decisions based upon their analysis. They take into account the library's circulation statistics, budget, and any gaps in specific subject areas. The Collection Development Department's plan should be directly related to the library system's goals and its mission statement.

Extension

The Extension Department is in charge of scheduling, maintaining, and driving the bookmobile. The bookmobile travels to various sections of the city or county that do not have a library nearby. The bookmobile also travels to nursing homes, day-care centers, and community centers. The stops are scheduled and the bookmobile is usually prompt to arrive and leave each stop. Some problems may be encountered when the bookmobile is out of order and patrons are waiting to pick up reserves or return books and materials.

In large library systems, the manager of this department oversees the operations of the branch libraries.

Human Resources

The Human Resources Department, also known as Personnel, handles issues dealing with staff. This department assists in hiring new staff and creating policies concerning staff performance evaluations, leave time, grievance procedures, and resignation. It also has charge of payroll. This is the department to contact when there are questions about job applications, interview scheduling, and verification of an employee's employment.

Local History Room

The Local History Room is where items of local interest are kept. It should contain a compilation of state and local history. Emphasis is placed on genealogy and the resources used to aid in a patron's search. Birth records, death records and books by and about people from your local area should be included. Very rarely do items from this collection circulate as it is not usually geared to casual browsers. It is generally for researchers interested in local history or tracing their family tree, or for a school assignment.

Periodicals

The Periodicals Department maintains the magazines and microforms owned by the library. There will be back issues of magazines as well as current issues. Microfilm and/or microfiche are housed by title and then by date. Printers and readers are nearby to use with the microform.

Public Relations

The Public Relations Department issues press releases, communicates with the media, and is a liaison between the library and the community. It handles the promotion of library services to the community. It is also in charge of publishing a calendar of events for the library system and ensuring that the library is involved in community-sponsored events.

Reader's Advisory

The Reader's Advisory Department helps patrons to find books that they would most like to read. If patrons have interests in specific authors, the Reader's Advisory staff can help patrons to find those authors and others who write in a similar style or genre. If patrons enjoy a specific genre, they can be directed to titles and authors of that genre. Also, if patrons love to read about specific plots, they can be directed to books that have those stories.

Technical Services

The Technical Services Department is where books and materials are cataloged and processed. When items are received from publishers and jobbers, they are verified against the packing slips and order forms. Items are cataloged, stamped with branch ownership, and then pockets and spine labels are added to link with the library's database. Some library systems receive their materials already processed. The Technical Services Department also receives materials back from branches that have cataloging or processing problems.

Training and Development

The Training and Development Department makes sure that all staff receive training and orientation for their new and current jobs. Many library systems require that new staff be trained at the main library. Other library systems allow staff to be trained at their new locations. The Training and Development Department also recruits professional representatives of companies to come to the library to do workshops for staff. This department seeks out and finds workshops offered at other locations that library staff are eligible to attend.

Young Adult

The Young Adult Department plans programs and suggests books to young adult patrons that they might enjoy. It may offer homework help or instruction on how to use the library. This department also gives tours to middle school and high school students. The Young Adult Department assists the Collection Development with suggested titles to order for young adults.

Library Vehicles

If you are part of a large library system, there may be vehicles available for staff to use when attending out-of-town workshops, doing off-site storytimes, and visiting other libraries. These vehicles are to be used only for library business. All library systems that use these vehicles should have procedures in place for employees to follow. You should request the use of a vehicle in advance so that the department in charge of scheduling the vehicles knows where they are at all times. The mileage, destination, staff member using the vehicle, date, and amount of gasoline used, should be logged every time the vehicle is used. These vehicles must be serviced regularly and filled up with gasoline.

If you request the use of a library vehicle, follow the established procedures. Find out what the procedure is in the event you are involved in a traffic accident while using the library vehicle. Do not run errands or have friends in the vehicle with you if they are not doing library business. If you plan to use the vehicle for an hour or less, it might be better to drive your own vehicle. Some library systems reimburse staff for using their own vehicles for library business. Try to request a vehicle only if you will need it for several hours or days.

3

Outside Support for the Library

Board of Trustees

Many county library facilities are governed by a Board of Trustees. The Board monitors the policies, expenses, and reports of all branches and the main library within the library system. Have a list of all current board members available at your branch. Patrons might want to contact them about a specific need they have or services they want to be made available. When you plan special programs like anniversary programs, invite the Board of Trustee members.

Friends of the Library

Many Libraries are supported by volunteer groups, usually called Friends of the Library.

Friends of Libraries U.S.A.

Friends of Libraries U.S.A. (FOLUSA) is a nationwide membership organization of local Friends groups, libraries, and individuals. This organization holds programs, lectures, author events, and exhibits. It publishes "News Update" (a bimonthly newsletter), Fact Sheets, educational videos for Friends, occasional special publications, and online toolkits to help libraries and Friends groups maximize support for libraries.

FOLUSA offers the Books for Babies program, which is aimed at putting books and library information in the hands of mothers and newborns. The organization also offers Literary Landmarks, a local development program that encourages communities to place identifying plaques on properties that are connected with famous authors. In addition, FOLUSA has award programs including $1000 annual prizes for six outstanding Friends groups; a $10,000 FOLUSA/Harper-Collins Publishers Award in honor of Barbara Kingsolver, given to a small public library with an exceptional Friends group; and special contests. FOLUSA also presents a Public Service Award to a public official for outstanding library support. Its networks include the State Friends organizations, Publishing Friends, and the FOLUSA-L electronic discussion group.

The mission of Friends of Libraries U.S.A. is to motivate and support local Friends groups across the country in their efforts to preserve and strengthen libraries, and to create awareness and appreciation of library services by:

- Assisting in developing Friends of the Library groups in order to generate local and state support.

- Providing guidance, education, and counsel throughout the Friends network.

- Promoting the development of strong library advocacy programs.

- Serving as a clearinghouse of information and expertise.

Visit the Friends of Libraries U.S.A. website at *www.folusa.org* for more information.

Books for Babies

This early childhood literacy program is used to promote reading, partnerships with other community groups, and library outreach. Visit the FOLUSA website at *www.folusa.org* and see the contents of their Books for Babies kits. The program's handy sheet of how-to tips will help your group create a successful project.

[Friends of Libraries U.S.A. website *www.folusa.org*. Reprinted with permission.]

Local Friends of the Library

Your local Friends of the Library group works to provide the library system with items not available through the library's budget. They provide money for programs, speakers, and training for library staff. The Friends of the Library also provide money for staff to attend state and national conferences. They typically organize book sales, which are their largest fundraisers.

Teen Friends

A good way to involve young people in the library is through a Friends of the Library group for teens. FOLUSA can help you to organize a teen friends of the library group.

1. First, decide on the library's goals for having the group. These could include: getting advice on planning buildings, interior design, services, and collections with appeal to teens; having teens participate directly in library programs and services; having teens help publicize library services among their peers; or a combination of these things. Second, the teens must choose

their own goals for the organization as well. A staff member or a volunteer will usually be the facilitator for the group and the liaison with the library.

2. Target age range: grades 7–12. Because teens change so rapidly, it may be desirable to target only early adolescents, or to have separate groups for younger and older teens.

3. Decide on the source(s) of funding: library budget, adult Friends group, dues, fundraising, etc.

4. Recruit members both formally through schools and other youth-serving organizations and through advertising and word-of-mouth from other teens. Hold an organizational meeting and have a staff member facilitate the group's choice of goals and activities. Set up a steering committee to help the teens decide how much structure they need to achieve their goals and help them create bylaws. Provide examples they can work from (available from Friends of Libraries U.S.A.)

5. The structure and bylaws will have established what kinds of officers or committees are needed. Assist the group in filling those positions.

6. Potential projects for Teen Friends include book discussion groups, program planning and performing, tutoring or story-telling for younger children, creating teen-oriented displays, creating a library newsletter, helping adult Friends with book sales, serving as Internet advisors/trainers, serving as library advocates, creating World Wide Web pages, participating in Internet book discussions, and assisting with a variety of short-term projects in the library.

7. Always keep the business portion of meetings brief.

8. Keep work and fun projects in balance.

9. Try whenever possible to have food available at meetings/projects. Teens always seem to work better and longer when food is available.

10. Do not let adults assume responsibility for planning. Teens will make decisions with the assistance of an adult facilitator, who can keep teens aware of available resources and limitations.

[Friends of Libraries U.S.A. website *www.folusa.org*. Reprinted with permission.]

4

The Library Administration and You

Always go through the proper channels when notifying the administration of specific situations at your branch. Never go directly "to the top" for situations that can be handled by other staff members within that department. Your first contact should always be your supervisor unless there are staff members in charge of specific projects. For example, if you need publicity for a program that you are having, call the public relations manager if there is one. After contacting that manager and exchanging information, send your boss an "FYI" (for your information). That way that person does not have to be involved in every aspect of your job but is kept informed about what you are doing.

Get to know everyone in the administration and develop a good relationship with them. Know what your boss and the administration expect from you. Respect their views and ways of doing things. Just because something was done one way where you were previously employed does not mean that it should be done the same way in this system. You need to be committed to your job as a manager. You were chosen to head a facility within the system that requires good leadership, good public relations, and the ability to provide quality service to the community. Seize the opportunity to prove to yourself and to others that you are ready to accept the challenge and will go above and beyond everyone's ideas of what is expected of you. Work every day as if your job depended on it. Don't start out strong and then fizzle out; start out strong and get stronger. Your branch and your employees will benefit from this.

Your Boss

Communication

You need to establish an open line of communication with your boss, who should always be kept informed of the good things going on at your branch as well as anything negative. If you have access to e-mail, use it. Don't let the boss find out about something that happened at your branch from someone else. If you are unsure about how to handle a situation, call your boss or another branch manager. This is especially true when dealing with patrons. If there is a situation at your branch that you don't think you can handle, offer the patron your boss's name and telephone number. If there is time, let your boss know to expect a telephone call and provide any needed information about the situation. Don't bombard your boss with every little problem that you could handle yourself, however. For example, do tell if you are planning a special storytime; but don't explain that you need someone to change the light bulbs unless the boss is the contact person for maintenance issues.

Chain of Command

In every library system there is a chain of command. The chain of command is the listing of library employees by their position in the system. When situations arise that you cannot handle yourself or if you need to inform the administration of something that happened, make sure that you follow the chain of command. Never skip over a member of the administration to try to speed up something that you want done. Your first contact should be your boss. If your boss is unavailable, then you should proceed to the next person on the list. Your boss will usually leave instructions for the staff as to whom to call when the boss is unavailable. You should never overlook your boss and go directly to a higher boss. How would you feel if your staff went directly to your boss with problems? It is not good when your boss knows more about your staff and what they are doing than you do.

Always try to see things from a different angle. If you are part of a large library system, your boss is probably the extension manager, with tremendous responsibilities. Your supervisor has many other branches to worry about, which may be why she can't spend all of her time telling you how to manage your branch. You are the branch manager and it is your responsibility to take care of your branch. The better you can handle situations at your branch, the easier your boss's job will be and the better your relationship with her. Also, your boss wants to see that you are able to take care of problems that arise at your branch—don't be so dependent that you are calling several times per day.

Offer to assist with other projects. If your boss asks for volunteers to help with various projects and you feel comfortable doing them, volunteer to help. Offer to have your staff assist at other branches. This gives them experience working at those other branches and it lets the administration know that you are a team player. You may need another branch to help you with staffing needs from time to time. If you have personal problems that interfere with your job performance, be candid with your boss. For example, instead of coming in to work late every morning, talk to your boss about any problems that prevent you from coming in at the scheduled time. Maybe your schedule can be adjusted so that you arrive a short time later but you stay later in the afternoon. Everything comes down to communication, because your boss can't read your mind.

Socializing with Your Boss

There will be times when social events are planned by or attended by your boss. Group events sponsored by the library or any of your colleagues are good ways to network and get to know librarians from other branches in your library system. Although you are at a social gathering, remember that your boss is still your boss and you shouldn't do or say anything inappropriate. Socializing with your boss gives you a chance to get to know him/her better. Talk to everyone at the gathering. Don't monopolize your boss's time by "sucking up" and talking about your branch the entire time. Also, don't use that time to complain about patrons, the library system, or your job. Try to talk about pleasant things and events.

It is not a good idea to socialize with your boss on an individual basis. I'm not talking about going out to lunch to talk about library issues. I am talking about seeing him/her after library hours. You don't want to appear to be doing anything inappropriate.

Your Performance Appraisal

Depending upon your library system's policy, you may have one or more performance appraisals during your first year as a branch manager. You may be appraised after a short probationary period to see how well you are performing your duties. Your boss will probably have a meeting with you to discuss your performance and any problems that should be corrected in the coming year. At that meeting, you should set goals and objectives for yourself that you plan to achieve. Performance appraisals can be stressful, but there should not be any information on the appraisal that you were not told before. If you have been having performance problems, your boss probably has spoken to you about them already. Talk to your boss about your job, and be honest about any fears you have and any assistance you think you need.

Don't be offended when your job performance is criticized. No one does everything right all the time. You will need guidance in your new position. Learn from your mistakes so they won't happen again. You will be appraised on your supervisory skills, customer service skills, and your ability to handle all of the paperwork required. Your boss's information will come from many sources. Although you are at a branch and he/she may be working at the main library, it will not be difficult for him/her to know how you are doing. For example, if your boss receives a lot of calls from patrons complaining about your branch and you in particular, that will have a negative impact on the customer-service portion of your appraisal. If your staff is always complaining to your boss about your attitude and he/she feels the complaints are justified, he/she is armed with more information to use on your appraisal. On the other hand, if the boss receives compliments from patrons and your staff is doing well, you will be seen as a manager with great customer-service and supervisory skills. Try to obtain a blank copy of the appraisal form before you are appraised so that you know what areas you will be appraised on. Don't be defensive; everyone gets evaluated. Use it as a tool to improve your performance. After reading and discussing the appraisal with your boss, keep a copy of it for your records.

Conflict

Your relationship with your boss can greatly influence your professional career. If you have a positive relationship with him/her you can learn a lot about being a supervisor, managing your branch, and solving patron problems. A negative relationship can stand in the way of your being able to thrive in a way that a branch manager should. Everyone deserves respect and you need to respect your boss even if you don't always agree on everything. Just as you want your employees to respect you, your boss also wants respect from you. If you have problems with your boss's behavior, handle the situation in a professional manner. Don't show disrespect for any reason, and don't judge your boss by what others say. You are hearing only one side of the story. Very few people will admit their shortcomings when they are angry with their boss. You may not agree with someone else's view. If you and your boss have differences of opinion, meet to resolve these differences. Make sure that you document everything that is said, and try to remain calm. Never get into a shouting match with your boss. If you cannot get along with your boss, talk to the human resources manager, who will let you know what the policy is regarding conflict management. Follow the policy procedures and make copies of any written reports.

5

Managing Yourself, Part 1: The Professional

Professionalism

Always be a professional. Once respect is lost, it is hard to regain. Enjoy your position and your staff but don't cross the line by telling dirty jokes, talking about people of different races, or demeaning yourself and others in any way. Inappropriate language such as swearing has no place in your vocabulary as a branch manager. Your inability to refrain from such behavior could have serious consequences. Your pride and commitment to your job are two very important aspects of being a great branch manager.

Dress for Success

When your appearance is on a professional level, you look and feel confident in yourself and your abilities. Patrons and the administration often come unannounced and want to have a meeting with you. Always look your best. Not only are you representing yourself, you also are representing your branch. Women should wear clean, neatly pressed outfits every day. Men should wear a tie every day. No tennis shoes, jeans, or dress-down days. Your branch is not at the forefront of any political and social agendas. T-shirts with slogans should not be worn. You may not have to buy a new wardrobe but as a branch manager you should dress as professionally as possible.

Networking

Network with your colleagues; you can learn a great deal from them. Go to lunch with one or more when you can. Call them when you have questions or are unsure about something. Visit other branches within the system. Talk to other managers about problems and/or successes at their branches. When attending conferences, start conversations with other branch librarians; their name tags will usually include their library affiliation and location. Get to know as many branch librarians as you can. You will be surprised how much you will learn about different branches just by talking to librarians from different states. Also, attend workshops specifically for branch managers.

Communication

Develop good communication skills. Your grammar in speech and print should always be professional. If you have problems communicating effectively, take an English or public speaking course. If you are bilingual, you have a special skill. You will be able to serve more patrons and develop programs to attract patrons who have language barriers. Offer classes in English as a second language at your branch for patrons who want to learn this language. Check with your local literacy agency to develop a partnership. Find out if any of your staff knows sign language and attend basic sign language workshops as they are offered.

Correspondence

Make sure that all correspondence sent from your branch looks professional. Typed memos and professional e-mails are the standard practice. Do not gossip through e-mail or printed correspondence. Gossiping is unprofessional and saying anything unkind about someone without being sure where that information will end up is risky. Make sure that all correspondence to your community or any outside organization is neatly typed on the library's letterhead. Check your grammar and spelling. Make sure all correspondence has your signature and position within the system. Ask the administration if you can have business cards printed. You may give them to patrons wanting to contact you at a later date. Also, when you are not at the branches, your staff can distribute them to patrons who may want to speak to you. Make sure that your business cards contain the library's logo, your name and position, and the name, address, telephone, and fax number of your branch. If you have an e-mail address include that as well.

Meetings

Be on time for meetings. Everyone has days when traffic is heavy or when their car is having problems, but being habitually late for meetings shows a lack of respect for those giving the meeting and is very unprofessional. Many times important information is addressed at the beginning of the meeting. You will miss those points if you are late. It is very disruptive, if someone is speaking to the group, when the door opens and everyone turns to see who is coming in. If any handouts were distributed before the latecomer arrived, others will scramble to make sure that all the material is provided. Also, the person sitting next to the latecomer will try to fill him in on what was said earlier, while missing what is currently being said. It takes up extra time and is not fair to those who arrived on time.

When attending meetings, make sure that you give the speaker your full attention. Sit as close to the speaker as possible and take notes if it is appropriate. Bring your planning calendar to record any announced upcoming events. Listen carefully to the speaker and to any questions being asked by the group. Don't ask the same question someone else just asked. Make good use of the meeting time, don't waste it.

Your Office

Always keep your office neat and organized. Although you may know where everything is, a messy office gives the impression that you are unorganized. You never know when you may have an unplanned meeting in your office. A nice plant, pictures on the wall, and a clean desk go a long way to boost self-esteem and encourage organization. Depending on the size of your office you may want to make sure you have some essential items. Try to have one or two chairs in your office for meetings with staff or patrons. Your desk should include a calendar, memo pad, to-do list, business cards, tissues, writing instruments, in and out baskets, an address file, and a telephone. Other items that you may want to include are a shelving unit against the wall, a file cabinet that locks, computer, printer, fax machine, shredder, and a comfortable desk chair. Of course not every branch is equipped with all of these items, but if your library has the budget for this type of equipment, you should request them. Your walls should display copies of your library degrees and any awards you have received related to your library career. You will need a bulletin board to post memos and telephone numbers to have handy.

If you are the manager of a small branch and you do not have your own office, make sure that your area allows you to have private conversations with your staff. It that is not possible, you may have to schedule private meetings in the morning before other staff arrives. If your desk is in the public area, make sure that it can be locked. If you manage a very small branch and have one or two staff members, you probably won't need a lot of the items mentioned above. Whether you manage a large branch or a small one, though, make sure you set aside an area in which to do your work and to be available for your staff. Always make sure that your desk is facing the door. Don't make your staff feel like you don't want to be bothered because your back is turned.

There is nothing wrong with displaying pictures of family or friends in your office. Just remember that you are at work and the number of photographs should be kept to a minimum—for example, one or two group pictures of your immediate family. You don't need to have pictures from every stage of your child's life on your desk. If you have more than one child, display a recent picture that includes all of them. A family portrait that includes all members of the family would be best.

Your Briefcase

You should invest in a nice briefcase or tote bag to store work that you take home each evening and bring to work each day. Your briefcase should hold your essential items and anything else that you think you may need to have available all the time. It should always contain the following items:

1. Your business cards.

2. Planner with a calendar. The planner with a calendar is important because it contains your library events and obligations. If you need to schedule

your child's school events you will know at a glance if there are any conflicts.

3. Staff and library system telephone numbers. If the weather takes an unexpected turn and the library is closed the next day, you want to be able to contact everyone to let them know.

4. Steno pads.

5. Writing instruments. The steno pad and pens are for when you go to meetings directly from home. You have the tools you need to take notes.

6. Paperwork that can be worked on in increments. The paperwork is for times when you are detained away from the branch—if you're stuck in traffic, for example. If you travel with your briefcase and are stuck with nowhere to go, you will have something worthwile you can accomplish.

7. Weekly schedule. The weekly schedule is great for when staff call you at home to tell you that they are sick and will not be in the next day. You know at a glance who else will be out that day, who is working the night shift or going to a workshop. I know before I leave home to go to work whether I need to call a substitute or if I think we have enough staff to work all service desks.

8. Cellular telephone. Your cellular telephone comes in handy in the detained situation because you can call your staff to let them know that you are stuck in traffic. You can also call if you are expected to be at a meeting and you know that you will either be late or not arrive at all.

9. A book, for those times when even the paperwork palls.

All of these items are important. I'm sure that there are other items that you would want to keep in your briefcase, as well, but these will meet most needs.

Professional Organizations

Part of being a professional is your membership in and knowledge of the appropriate organizations and publications. For Librarians, the primary professional organization is the ALA.

American Library Association (ALA)

The American Library Association (ALA) was founded in 1876 in Philadelphia and subsequently chartered in the Commonwealth of Massachusetts. Its mission is "to provide leadership for the development, promotion, and improvement of library and information services and the profession of librarianship in order to enhance learning and ensure access to information for all." Its membership is open to "any person, library, or other organization interested in library service and librarianship … upon payment of the dues provided for in the Bylaws."

It is governed by an elected Council, its policy-making body, and an Executive Board which "acts for the Council in the administration of established policies and programs." Policies and programs are proposed by standing committees, designated as committees of the Association or committees of Council. Headquartered in Chicago, its operations are directed by an Executive Director and implemented by staff through a structure of programmatic offices and support units.

ALA is home to eleven membership divisions, each focused on a type of library or type of library function. It also includes round tables, groups of members "interested in the same field of librarianship not within the scope of any division." A network of affiliates, chapters and other organizations enables ALA to reach a broad audience.

DIVISIONS OF ALA

ALA divisions publish journals, books, newsletters and other materials; provide continuing education in a variety of venues and formats; offer awards and scholarships; sponsor institutes and conferences; and maintain networks of affiliates, chapters and other collaborative relationships.

Members of ALA divisions must first be members of the American Library Association. A majority of ALA members belong to one or more division.

ALA divisions include:

- American Association of School Librarians (AASL)
- Association for Library Collections and Technical Services (ALCTS)
- Association for Library Service to Children (ALSC)
- Association for Library Trustees and Advocates (ALTA)
- Association of College and Research Libraries (ACRL)
- Association of Specialized and Cooperative Library Agencies (ASCLA)
- Library Administration and Management Association (LAMA)
- Library and Information Technology Association (LITA)
- Public Library Association (PLA)
- Reference and User Services Association (RUSA)
- Young Adult Library Services Association (YALSA)

[American Library Association website *www.ala.org*. Reprinted with permission.]
Attend library conferences to learn more about the library profession. Become a member of your state's library association and the American Library Association.

Attend both conferences when you can. You will learn a lot about library service and can network with librarians from other states. Visit the exhibits to see what is new and upcoming. Talk to the exhibitors; they will be more than happy to talk to you about their products. You can pick up lots of free posters, bags, pencils, and other items. A very exciting part of the ALA conference is that you get to meet many authors and illustrators. They are there to talk to you or to autograph copies of their book. I have autographed copies of books from such authors and illustrators as Mildred Taylor, Rosa Parks, Tom Feelings, Brian Pinkney, Ann Cameron and many more. The conferences are held in large cities and you can visit the local attractions while you are there. It is a great experience that I highly recommend. Membership forms are available on their website at ww.ala.org and also by writing them at ALA 50 E. Huron Street, Chicago, IL 60611.

MEDALS AWARDED BY THE AMERICAN LIBRARY ASSOCIATION

The ALA gives out many awards recognizing excellence in various aspects of books and libraries. Here are but a few of the best known, relating to children's literature.

John Newbery Medal

The Newbery Medal is awarded annually by the American Library Association for the most distinguished American children's book published the previous year. On June 21, 1921, Frederic G. Melcher proposed the award to the American Library Association meeting of the Children's Librarians' Section and suggested that it be named for the eighteenth-century English bookseller John Newbery. The idea was enthusiastically accepted by the children's librarians, and Melcher's official proposal was approved by the ALA Executive Board in 1922. In Melcher's formal agreement with the board, the purpose of the Newbery Medal was stated as follows: "To encourage original creative work in the field of books for children. To emphasize to the public that contributions to the literature for children deserve similar recognition to poetry, plays, or novels. To give those librarians, who make it their life work to serve children's reading interests, an opportunity to encourage good writing in this field."

The Newbery Award thus became the first children's book award in the world. Its terms, as well as its long history, continue to make it the best known and most discussed children's book award in this country.

Randolph Caldecott Medal

Each year the Newbery Medal is awarded by the American Library Association for the most distinguished American children's books published the previous year. However, as many persons became concerned that the artists creating picture books for children were as deserving of honor and encouragement as were the authors of children's books, Frederic G. Melcher suggested in 1937 the establishment of a second annual medal. This medal is to be given to the artist who had created the most distinguished picture book of the year and named in honor of the nineteenth-century English illustrator Randolph J. Caldecott. The idea for this medal was also accepted enthusiastically by the Section for Library Work with Children of ALA and was approved by the ALA Executive Board.

The Caldecott Medal "shall be awarded to the artist of the most distinguished American Picture Book for Children published in the United States during the preceding year. The award shall go to the artist, who must be a citizen or resident of the United States, whether or not he be the author of the text. Members of the Newbery Medal Committee will serve as judges. If a book of the year is nominated for both the Newbery and Caldecott Awards the committee shall decide under which heading it shall be voted upon, so that the same title shall not be considered on both ballots." In 1977 the Board of Directors of the Association for Library Service to Children rescinded the final part of the 1937 action and approved that "any book published in the preceding year shall be eligible to be considered for either award or both awards." Separate committees to choose the Newbery and Caldecott Awards were established in 1977.

From the beginning of the award of the Newbery and Caldecott Medals, committees could, and usually did, cite other books as worthy of attention. Such books were referred to as Newbery of Caldecott "runners-up." In 1971 the term "runners-up" was changed to "honor books." The new terminology was made retroactive so that all former runners-up are now referred to as Newbery or Caldecott Honor Books.

Coretta Scott King Award

The Coretta Scott King Award is presented annually by the Coretta Scott King Task Force of the American Library Association's Social Responsibilities Round Table. Recipients are authors and illustrators of African descent whose distinguished books promote an understanding and appreciation of the "American Dream."

The Award commemorates the life and work of Dr. Martin Luther King Jr., and honors his widow, Coretta Scott King, for her courage and determination in continuing the work for peace and world brotherhood. Winners of the Coretta Scott King Award receive a framed citation, an honorarium, and a set of *Encyclopedia Britannica* or *World Book Encyclopedia*.

Coretta Scott King Award books are chosen by a seven-member national award jury. The CSK Award Jury also chooses the winners of the John Steptoe Award for New Talent. These books affirm new talent and offer visibility to excellence in writing or illustration at the beginning of a career as a published book creator.

John Steptoe Award for New Talent

The John Steptoe Award for New Talent, given to a black author and to a black illustrator for an outstanding book, is designed to bring visibility to a writer or artist at the beginning of his/her career as a published book creator. The award is presented annually for text or illustrations. The Committee may choose to select one book for writing and a second book for illustration. The John Steptoe Award for New Talent was presented for the first time in 1995.

The Michael L. Printz Award

The Michael L. Printz Award is an award for a book that exemplifies literary excellence in young adult literature. It is selected annually by an award committee that can also name as many as four honor books. The award-winning book can be fiction, nonfiction, poetry or an anthology, and can be a work of joint authorship or editorship. The books must be published between January 1 and December 31 of the preceding year and be designated by the publisher as being either a young adult book or one published for the age range that YALSA defines as young adult, i.e., ages 12 through 18.

This award "serves notice on the reading, publishing, and bookselling communities that young adult literature has come of age," says Michael Cart, Chair of the Best Young Adult Book Award Feasibility Task Force. The task force laid the groundwork for the award that was approved by the YALSA Board in January, 1999.

The Mildred L. Batchelder Award

This award honors Mildred L. Batchelder, a former executive director of the Association for Library Service to Children, a believer in the importance of good books for children in translation from all parts of the world. Batchelder spent 30 years with ALA, working as an ambassador to the world on behalf of children and books, encouraging and promoting the translation of the world's best children's literature. Her life's work was "to eliminate barriers to understanding between people of different cultures, races, nations, and languages."

This award, established in her honor in 1966, is a citation awarded to an American publisher for a children's book considered to be the most outstanding of those books originally published in a foreign language in a foreign country, and subsequently translated into English and published in the United States. ALSC gives the award to encourage American publishers to seek out superior children's books abroad and to promote communication among the peoples of the world.

The Laura Ingalls Wilder Medal

Administered by the Association for Library Service to Children, a division of the American Library Association, the Laura Ingalls Wilder Award was first given to its namesake in 1954. The award, a bronze medal, honors an author or illustrator whose books, published in the United States, have made, over a period of years, a substantial and lasting contribution to literature for children.

The Pura Belpré Award

The Pura Belpré Award, established in 1966, is presented to a Latino/Latina writer and illustrator whose work best portrays, affirms,

and celebrates the Latino cultural experience in an outstanding work
of literature for children and youth. It is co-sponsored by the Association for Library Service to Children (ALSC), a division of the American Library Association (ALA) and the National Association to Promote Library and Information Services to Latinos and the
Spanish-Speaking (REFORMA), an ALA Affiliate.

The award is named after Pura Belpré, the first Latina librarian
from the New York Public Library. As a children's librarian, storyteller, and author, she enriched the lives of Puerto Rican children in
the U.S.A. through her pioneering work of preserving and disseminating Puerto Rican folklore. The award is given biennially.

The Andrew Carnegie Medal for Excellence in Children's Video

The Andrew Carnegie Medal for Excellence in Children's Video,
supported by the Carnegie Corporation of New York, was awarded
for the first time in 1991 to honor outstanding video productions for
children released during the previous year. The annual award is given
to the video's producer by the Association for Library Service to
Children (ALSC), a division of ALA, through a Carnegie endow-
ment.

Video productions which receive the Andrew Carnegie Medal meet
criteria which include the following: they show respect for a child's
intelligence and imagination, and reflect and encourage children's interests; they take advantage of the special techniques of the medium,
including visuals, voices, music, language, and sound effects; and, if
adaptations of materials originally produced in other mediums, they
remain true to, expand, or complement the work. Only entries originally released in the United States, and produced by a U.S. citizen or
resident or by a company headquartered in the U.S. are eligible.

[Source: American Library Association website *www.ala.org*.
Reprinted with permission.]

Professional Journals

Read professional journals to keep up with what is going on in the library
world. Journals such as *Library Journal*, *Library Hotline*, *American Libraries*, and others will let you know what other libraries are doing. Many other professional library
publications review books prior to publication as well as recently published titles.
They will be essential if you are acquiring new books for your library.

6

Managing Yourself, Part 2: The Worker

Time Management

Managing your time wisely can save you a lot of time and you can get much more accomplished. You need to set specific goals and objectives for what you want and need to accomplish within a given time period. On your daily to-do list, prioritize your duties. Do the most important work first. Begin early in the morning when your brain is not yet cluttered with events of the day. If it helps you work better, close your office door. I'm sure your staff will understand if you let them know that you are working on a project that must be completed without interruptions.

Some days you will notice that although you have a to-do list and you are concentrating on getting your work done, at the end of the day you have not accomplished as much as you wanted to. One reason may be constant interruptions. You will be surprised how much time is spent during interruptions. You want to be approachable and have your staff come to you, but not to the point where your office door is a revolving one. When a staff member asks to speak to you because of a concern that they have, ask them if they have spoken to their direct supervisor. If you have department managers at your branch they should be the first to deal with employee concerns. If you are the only supervisor at your branch, you will have to resolve the problem or clarify the policy or procedure. If someone wants to tell you a joke or talk about social matters, you can politely tell them that you would love to talk but you really have to finish what you are doing. Later on if you have a break you can ask them what they wanted to talk about. It is a difficult situation because the more you are interrupted the more comfortable your staff feels in coming in and talking to you. The problem comes when they want to do it all the time. You don't want to be in a situation where you are never interrupted because your staff don't feel you are approachable. If they don't ever come to you, that means that they are making decisions on their own whether they are the right ones or not. Try to strike a balance so that you and your staff have a good relationship, but you are also able to get your work done.

Some Time-Management Techniques

1. Learn to say no. When you are truly too busy, it's usually the best thing to do.

2. Set the parameters. If you can't complete a new project by the deadline, say so.

3. Get up an hour earlier. You will accomplish a lot more when there are fewer distractions at home.

4. Stay seated when you are working on a project. The moment you stand up, there is an opportunity for you to be distracted by something else.

5. Design a productive workspace. Have everything within easy reach.

6. Determine priorities.

7. Have a starting and ending time for all meetings that you conduct.

Plan

The more plans you make and the earlier you make them, the easier your job will be. This applies to paperwork, programming, meetings, and training new staff. Purchase steno pads or ledgers to take notes while you plan. When planning programs, start as early as possible. Two months ahead is not too early to plan a large program such as a children's festival. When planning, delegate duties to different people so that no one person has total responsibility for everything. When training new staff members, plan who will do the training and when. Everyone, including patrons, will be able to tell when an event is well planned. It will be organized and everything will flow smoothly. When planning a meeting, think about what your agenda will include and who should attend. If appropriate, share the agenda with attendees ahead of time. And, during the meeting, stick to that agenda.

Keep All Memos

In the age of new technology, many memos may be in the form of e-mail. We can send e-mail and attachments to the entire library system in a matter of minutes. Don't delete important e-mails right after reading them. If your boss sends you an e-mail detailing a report to be submitted, do write the due date in your planner but don't delete any instructions; you may need to refer to them later when you are working on your report. When reading e-mails quickly, you might miss the important parts. Rereading later ensures that you completely understand the memo. If your boss gives you approval for a specific item that you want to purchase for your library, the e-mail is written confirmation and proof that your item was approved. If you want to delete those messages because your mailbox is getting full, print off a copy and file it for future reference.

Read all memos thoroughly. When you receive mail, if you don't have time to read it right away, leave it on top of your desk so that you can read it later the same day.

Be Prepared for Reports

Begin working on projects right away. As soon as you receive a memo that something is due on a certain date, first record it in your planner and then begin to work on it as soon as you can. If you are required to write monthly narratives of the happenings at your branch, each day record anything going on that you would like to mention in your report. That way when it is time to compile your report, the notes will be readily available, and you won't be wondering what happened last month. For example, I record notes on my desk calendar. The microfilm machine was repaired, the air conditioner was serviced, the lawn was mowed, we held an Internet instruction class, etc. Don't put off noting events, because you may receive another report in the meantime. If you held a storytime, record the name of the group and the total in attendance. The more notes you take, the more accurate your monthly narrative will be.

Write everything down. Don't depend on your memory. Everyone forgets things now and then. Don't let it be an important meeting that you forgot to attend. Use a weekly/monthly planner and record all deadlines and events for work and personal activities. That way you won't have to look in two different places. You will know at a glance everything that you need to take care of that week and that month—reports due, staff vacations, personal appointments. Take it wherever you go. Take it to meetings so that you can record the next meeting's date.

Make a list. Always keep a list of things to do on top of your desk. Every time you complete a task, mark it off of your list. This lets you know how much you are accomplishing on a given day. Try to accomplish as much as you can without sacrificing the quality of your work. Don't rush through a job just to finish it and mark it off of your list, however. If you submit poor quality work, I assure you that you will see it again.

Delegate reports to employees who will complete them on time. You are ultimately responsible for whatever leaves your branch no matter who completed it. Look over all reports before they are submitted. You wouldn't want to have to answer questions about a report that you never looked at.

Overcome Procrastination

Why do people put off doing things until the last minute? Some people claim to work better under pressure. Why add stress to your life by waiting and possibly not making your deadline because of unforeseen circumstances? The day before something is due you could be sick or have a family emergency. Employers are usually sensitive to personal problems, but if you were given weeks to complete a project that should have taken only days and you request an extension because of your emergency, your boss will know that you procrastinated. Most people who procrastinate do it for several reasons. The most common reason is fear. Here are some ideas to help overcome your natural tendency to procrastinate.

- Give yourself new deadlines. Pretend that the deadline for your report is a week earlier than it actually is.

- Make it a personal rule not to take work home. If you know that you will be taking work home you won't try hard to finish it all at the library. When you get home, you may be tired, have other things to do, and procrastinate yet again. You will promise yourself to do your work the next day.

- Don't do any work on the weekends. You need quiet time to yourself.

Some other ways to overcome procrastination include the following:

1. Stick to your to-do list and break up your tasks into increments.
2. Start with the task that you would most like to do.
3. When you finally complete that difficult task, do something fun as a reward.
4. Don't be a perfectionist. Do the best you can without stressing over it.
5. Delegate jobs that you know can be completed by a competent staff member.
6. Don't waste time with unimportant tasks.
7. Focus on your tasks and limit outside distractions.
8. Use technology to help with your tasks. Computers are great time savers. (But be careful: they can also be great time wasters.)
9. Don't begin working on projects that you think your boss might give you. The project may get assigned to someone else or the boss might change her mind about doing the project.

Stress

Stress can come from many different factors. You may be overworked or not have enough work to do. There may be many deadlines that you have to meet. If you can't cope effectively with the stressors in your life, it could have a negative effect on your health and personality. Excessive stress could affect your ability to make the best decisions. It can also cause you to have poor relationships with the people around you. In addition to job stress, there may be other things and relationships that cause stress in your life. Money problems, rearing children, and just daily tasks to take care of can cause stress. Identify those stressors so that you can adequately deal with them. Excessive stress can cause headaches, high pulse rates, high blood pressure and cholesterol, ulcers, and heart disease. Stress will sometimes cause you to have lower self esteem and motivation.

Some people deal with stress by excessive drinking, excessive eating, taking excessive sick days, and quitting their jobs. Instead, try to relax. Take a yoga class or try meditation. You can meditate in your car or any quiet place where you can be alone. Sometimes a good cry will make you feel better. Go out with family or friends who make you feel good about yourself. Develop a hobby. Treat yourself to a massage. Have a day all to yourself doing exactly what you want to do. Make a list of guilty pleasures to choose from on those days when you feel you need one. Some guilty pleasures may include:

1. A long, hot bubble bath.
2. Watching a funny movie and laughing out loud.
3. Going window-shopping with friends.
4. Singing in the shower.
5. Buying or fixing a delicious dessert and eating all of it.

Every time you think of something that would be nice for you to do once in a while, add it to your list. Listen to an audio book in your car while you commute to and from work. It will keep you from worrying about other things in your life. Talk to your doctor about an exercise plan that is right for you. Exercise helps you to burn calories, lower your stress level, and improve your mood.

If you feel you must worry, set aside half an hour per day just to worry. Just write in your planner that at 7:00 P.M. each day you will worry. It seems silly but it does work. Soon you will forget about worrying during that time period.

If none of the above suggestions help, find out if your library system offers its employees confidential counseling through the employee assistance program (EAP). It has trained licensed counselors to talk with you about your problems and to help you to find solutions.

Anger Management

Know how to handle your anger. When staff or patrons make you angry, pause and mentally count to ten if you feel you will say something that you will regret. Make sure that the words that come out of your mouth are those that you intended to say. Once something is said, no amount of apologies can change it. It is better to be silent than to risk alienating your employees. Talking down to people never encourages them, it only reduces motivation and respect for you. Respect is your reputation. Once lost, it takes years to regain, if it ever is. People remember being mistreated for a long time. I often hear people talk about losing respect for people because of something that person did or said five, sometimes ten, years ago. Think about someone who said something to you that you didn't like. Do you feel the same way about that person as you did before they said it? Before you do or say something to your staff that criticizes them or their performance in an abusive way, ask yourself this question, "Would I want my boss to treat me that way?" If the answer is no, then handle the situation differently. There is often a better way to do or say something.

Be calm. Don't make employees afraid of you. Threats and intimidation do not scare employees into doing their jobs. You are a supervisor, not a warden in a prison. Do you think that you would do a good job if your boss threatened to fire you or made you feel inadequate? Everyone knows that you are in charge. Only a supervisor with low self-confidence tries to bully their staff into performing. People work better when they are relaxed. Ideas flow much more easily. If your staff feels that they can come and talk to you no matter how far-fetched the idea, you have a good relationship with them.

Learn to let things go. Not every situation needs to be treated like a major catastrophe. If a minor situation occurs with an employee, after you have spoken to them about it let it go. Don't keep bringing up the same situation over and over. For example, if an employee is scheduled to go to a workshop but forgets to attend, don't prevent them from attending future workshops. Don't tell that person that you will allow them to go only if they don't forget to go this time. Let it go. No one is perfect. If another staff member asks to go to a workshop, don't say, "Write it down. I don't want you to forget to attend the way Bob did."

Meditation

1. Find a quiet place where you can be by yourself and avoid interruptions.

2. Set a timer or alarm clock for 20 minutes, so that you don't have to worry about keeping track of time.

3. Loosen any clothing that is tight or uncomfortable.

4. Sit in a comfortable position or lie down on the floor, a couch, or a bed, placing a pillow or cushion under your head.

5. Close your eyes and try to concentrate on something that is pleasing to you. You will probably find that your brain is capable of focusing on a relaxing thought and still be carrying on a conversation about something else, or you may find that your brain is focusing on your breathing or on how your arm feels. Don't worry; just gently push that thought out of your mind, telling yourself that you will deal with it later. Return to your relaxing thought. If a relaxing thought doesn't seem to be working, try repeating a special word (something or someone you like), or even just a syllable, such as "om." You can say it softly aloud if that helps, especially if you are just getting started with meditation. As you become more practiced in meditation, you will find that mind wandering disappears.

6. Gradually you will feel relaxed, calm, and refreshed. When the alarm or timer sounds, open your eyes and slowly bring yourself back into your surroundings. Don't jump up right away and plunge back into your work! Stretch a little, yawn if you feel like it, and give yourself a pat on the back for taking such good care of yourself. Don't worry if you don't notice

tremendous results right away. Relaxation will come the more you practice meditation.

Be patient with meditating. Most new users find that it takes a week or two before they begin to experience deep relaxation and rejuvenation. So stick with it, even if it doesn't seem to be doing you much good right away.

You should strive to stay in good health. Visit your doctor regularly, eat nutritious foods, and get plenty of sleep. If you feel good you can make better decisions and are less likely to react to stress with anger.

7

Effective Supervision

There are many qualities that are essential to being an effective supervisor. Whether you have these qualities or not will determine the type of supervisor you will be. It will also determine whether your job is rewarding or just a constant struggle. First, you need to have a positive attitude. You must believe that you can handle any situation that presents itself. Be confident in your abilities and be able to grow with each new experience. Read books and articles on supervision and management. Write down anything you read that can be incorporated into your job. Attend workshops on supervision and network with colleagues to discuss various issues that they deal with. Talk to supervisors with both large and small staffs to get a perspective on the differences and the similarities of staffs of various sizes. In addition, talk to supervisors who have been in the system five years or more. Ask them what works and what doesn't. Ask your boss to suggest the names of colleagues in the system for you to network with. Those people are the individuals whose management styles your boss admires.

Love your job. You're a branch manager! I'm sure that you worked very hard to achieve this goal. Don't see each day as a challenge. Enjoy your new position as you settle into the world of professional librarians. Relax. Don't make your employees feel that you are incompetent because you are nervous about your job. Don't second-guess yourself. Think about what decisions should be made and make them. On the other hand, don't feel pressured into making snap decisions. Snap decisions usually end up being wrong decisions.

Attitude

Try to have the same attitude all the time. Don't be in a bad mood one day and in a good mood the next. Your staff need to know what to expect when they talk to you. It is hard to supervise employees who think their supervisor is unpredictable. They will withdraw from you for fear of embarrassment or humiliation. If you find that you are always moody, try talking to a professional to see what is the underlying cause. Don't risk damaging your reputation as a professional because you are too embarrassed to seek professional help. It will probably make you a better person and a more effective manager.

Attitude is extremely important to good supervision. Managers have the proper attitude if they do the following:

1. Manage with a high degree of integrity and lead by example;
2. Keep their word to employees;
3. Earn the respect, trust, and confidence of employees;
4. Strive to help employees develop to their full potential;
5. Give credit to employees who do a good job;
6. Accept higher-level decisions and directives and demonstrate this to employees;
7. Refrain from discussing personal feelings about library administration with employees;
8. Discuss disagreements with library administration privately;
9. Be responsible for the performance of their employees;
10. Be objective in judging the actions of employees;
11. Decide matters involving employees on the basis of facts and circumstances, not personal sympathies;
12. Accept the responsibility for rehabilitating rather than punishing employees whenever possible;
13. Be prepared to support employees in cases where they are in the right;
14. Allow employees to have as much control over their own work as possible; and
15. Work to maintain a workplace climate that allows employees to express their feelings and concerns openly without fear of reprisal.

Individuals charged with the responsibility of supervising one volunteer or 25 librarians need essentially the same basic supervisory skills. It is easy to underestimate the value and impact of volunteer supervision. On the one hand, it can provide valuable supervisory experience, which, if done well, can prepare one for higher-level supervision. On the other hand, if done poorly, it can have a negative effect on volunteers, for many of whom this is a first volunteer experience. Libraries must recognize that assigning supervisory responsibilities to an individual carries with it the obligation to help him or her learn and develop the skills needed to do the job right.

[*Whole Library Handbook 3*; by George Eberhart. Reproduced with permission.]

A smile goes a long way. Not a phony smile, but a genuine "I care about you" smile. Allow your staff to get to know you. A phony person can be seen a mile away. If you genuinely cannot get along with people and feel you must always be in control, maybe this career is not for you. Take a look at yourself and think about what really makes you happy. You must be happy with your career to be fulfilled and to have a positive attitude.

Be a leader. Don't rush to the telephone to call someone else when issues arise. Let your staff see that you are able to take charge of any situation. If staff come to you about a patron that they can't handle, tell them that you will take care of it. If a patron calls and gives a staff member a hard time, offer to talk to the patron but don't just take over the situation. Ask your employee if he would like you to talk to the patron. If you witness a transaction between patron and staff where the patron is getting irritated, walk over to your staff and ask them if they need your assistance. If they say that they can handle it, walk away and allow them to do so. Give your staff the option to call you when they need you or to take care of the situation themselves.

Try to be as flexible as possible with employees while still meeting the needs of your branch. Read your system's policy on specific types of leave and employee rights. The educational goals of your employees may determine how much, if any, time off is given. If someone is attending library school to improve their skills in order to apply for a professional position, you may want to arrange the schedule so that they can work and attend classes. For example, if you have an employee in graduate school and they would like to take a reference course either in the morning or late afternoon, try to work your schedule around their class. Have someone else work the service desk when their class is in session and schedule them on the desk at another time. The small inconvenience of rescheduling will be made up for by an employee with more training and education. They will have ideas and insights on new and upcoming technologies.

Don't discuss any negative feelings you have about your boss or the administration with your staff. Your negative feelings will transfer to them and you don't want your branch to be unable to communicate effectively with the library administration.

Listen to employees who say good things about their supervisors. What are they saying? What makes their supervisor different from others? Different from you? Don't criticize or be jealous of good managers. Be one of them! You know that you are a good manager if one manager resigns and the staff calls you and asks if you would apply for the new position. Word has spread that you are a great person to work for.

Supervising Your Friends

I have been placed in the position several times of supervising my friends. This happened when we were all library assistants while I was attending library school.

After I graduated and was offered a supervisory position, I realized that I would be supervising many of my friends and coworkers. Rather than making abrupt changes overnight and treating my new staff differently, I took the gradual approach. I continued to have lunch with them but I made sure that we returned to work on time. If they did or said something against policy, I would encourage them not to and I would tell them the proper procedure. They knew that I understood the concerns and problems they had with the library system. I wasn't someone new coming in who didn't know them or the job. Gradually my role changed; although we were still friends, I went to lunch with them less often and I didn't converse with them as much because they knew that I had a lot of work to do. I gave them a lot of respect and in turn I was given respect. In fact, I could ask my new employees to do things that they never would have done for a previous or new supervisor. I didn't ask them to do anything that I wouldn't do myself and they knew that. They found themselves volunteering for what they considered to be unimportant jobs because they were made to feel that all jobs were important, especially if the supervisor did them. If your employees feel that every job is important, no matter how small, they will feel better about themselves and their work. Don't make the mistake of being their friend one day and their tyrant boss the next. Be a boss without being bossy. Treat all of your employees the same. Don't show any favoritism toward employees whom you consider to be friends. Everyone will adjust to your new status and you will too.

Management Styles

What type of manager are you? Are you directional? If so, your management style is one of just telling people what to do. You delegate many tasks and expect your staff to do them without question. You feel that since you are in charge, you know what is best for your branch and your staff. You are not very approachable because your staff is either intimidated or frightened by you. You like it that way because you have more control over what goes on at your branch. You micromanage because you want to make sure that your staff does everything you want them to do, the way you want them to do it. You don't understand why staff don't tell you what is going on with their lives or things that happen at the branch in your absence. You think that you are a great manager because, although you don't work the service desk yourself, you have read books and attended workshops so you know how things should be done. You assume that if a patron is unhappy it must be because of something your staff did wrong. If staff followed the rules of good customer service, everyone should leave happy. You don't listen to anything your staff has to say because they are subordinates and they couldn't possibly know as much as you do about the library. You don't understand why you keep having vacancies but you assume it is because those employees just did not have what it took to do their jobs effectively.

Is your management style democratic? If so, you actively seek your staff's input in making decisions that affect everyone at the branch. Your staff meetings are inclusive and everyone's thoughts are heard. You spend a great deal of time listening to your staff. You compromise in situations where there is a disagreement between you and one of your employees. You see your branch as a team effort rather than a boss with his/her staff in subordinate positions. You perform all duties at your branch for several reasons:

1. To make sure that you can suggest changes in procedures because you know what the current procedures are.

2. To allow your staff to see that you are a team player and you will not ask them to do something that you would not do yourself.

3. To be able to answer patron complaints when they need clarification about why we do certain things.

You are very approachable and have an individual relationship with each one of your staff members. There are many ways to accomplish this. You work at the service desks at different times of the day. Sooner or later you will work with everyone. You talk about things other than their jobs. If you have something in common with them, children for instance, you talk about some of the funny stories involving them. Not only does your staff feel more at ease with you, but they also see you as a human being and not just a manager.

Both of these management styles exist in every library system. The best management style would be a combination of the two. You need to be directional when you have a difficult staff member who needs to be told what to do sometimes. Also, if there is an emergency at the branch and there is no time to talk to staff, tell them what you want them to do. When the crisis is over, explain why certain actions were taken. That way, when you are not there, they will act appropriately. You should encourage your staff to make their own decisions but they need to know that you can make changes to their decisions if necessary. If you involve your staff in the decision-making process, they have a more positive attitude toward their jobs. This does not mean that every decision you make should involve your staff. Day-to-day routine decisions should be made by you. Decisions such as programming, new procedures, and handling problem patrons should be discussed with staff.

The following Top-Ten lists were developed by one library, but can be applied to all.

Supervising Library Paraprofessionals

Paraprofessionals, or "paras," are your nonprofessional staff members.

Top Ten Things NOT TO DO When Supervising

10. **Don't pile on assignment after assignment.** Give staff time to re-coup before starting another project. It is disheartening to assign another project, before the first one is finished. Ensure the staff is clear in your expectations. Don't throw your work onto the nearest para to you.

9. **Don't break a confidence.** When someone speaks to you in private keep it private. Your staff needs to know that they can trust you and that you will show them respect. If they express something you would like to share ask permission; if it is not given, keep your conversation private.

8. **Don't play favorites.** Playing favorites is counteractive to teamwork. View all your staff as individuals with different talents and abilities. Playing favorites breeds discontentment. Be fair and honest in your dealings. Don't change the rules for one and not the others, except for the occasional time an individual may have a personal crisis.

7. **Don't be overly critical.** Practice patience—people do things in different ways. When they are doing the very best they can, recognize the efforts put forth.

6. **Don't be insincere.** Admit mistakes. Don't grovel or whine or make excuses. Don't blame your tools or equipment. Whatever you do don't blame your staff. We all fuss some times, but don't make it a habit. Also, we want to be honest in our praise. Mean what you say.

5. **Don't expect paras to run your personal errands.** Never! Never! Never! Don't ask them to go to the cleaners for you or to purchase snacks for you while they are on their breaks or on the way to or from work. Paras are not inferior or underlings to you and are not your errand boys.

4. **Don't expect more from paras than you do of yourself.** They are workers also and on the same team as yourself. Don't prejudge what paras can do. Don't expect your paras to be more human or superhuman in tasks given or performed. Don't request your support staff to do the jobs you do not like to do.

3. **Don't demand "your way."** Try to always give choices. Remember that different people have different work styles. Some need a little extra assistance or training. Most staff will be happier, as well as more productive, when they are given a chance to use their own abilities.

2. **Don't have an "us" versus "them" attitude.** We are all working toward one goal—to provide services to our patrons. You don't have to have a M.L.S. to be "professional" in your job. At times we do not get the respect or acknowledgment we deserve, but

when we are doing our best, we can at least feel good about ourselves. As long as we know we are doing "professional" work, our self-esteem for a job well done should make us better employees. It is all an attitude. WE ARE PROFESSIONAL.

1. **Don't micromanage.** Don't manage or control with excessive attention to minor details. Provide clear instructions, training, materials, and equipment and let the paras do their job. Offer assistance when requested in an attitude of mutually respectful professionalism. Be aware of what is going on in each department. But do not hover, nag, sneak peeks at work in progress, or otherwise distract the paraprofessional and give the impression that you do not trust his or her ability to do the job. If you are a worrywart, set times for progress checks weekly, etc., but don't show disrespect by looking over shoulders, irritating and discouraging your support staff.

Top Ten Things TO DO When Supervising

10. **Be an active listener.** Make communication top priority. Listen to what they are saying and what they are not saying. Listen to body language.

9. **Be a friendly mentor.** Be open and available to staff. Let them know they can approach you with a concern. Learn to know each para's strengths and utilize them to the max. Know who are self-motivators and who need help in setting priorities. Set a good example. Don't use your paras as sounding boards for your personal life. "Start as a friendly mentor and end as a friendly professional colleague."

8. **Recognize and reward special efforts.** Samples of recognition: "Applause," "Courtesy," "Seal of Approval," and the "Employee of the month" awards. Don't forget the "Thank you."

7. **Share successes—take failures onto yourself.** Promote your staff whenever possible. Talk about the good things they are doing. An example might be, "We all worked together to make this task or program successful." Be loyal to your support staff and don't blame them for failures.

6. **Encourage continuing education.** Stress the importance of good education. Be sure to inform the staff of library education opportunities. Stress professional growth and personal goal setting.

5. **Arrange for one or more paras to attend training.** Encourage paras to attend programs, workshops, and conferences. If the conference is close and it is possible, try to share conferences (a day or two). Encourage them to share with the rest of staff what they have learned and bring back handouts whenever possible. Provide training when it is needed. The "Soaring to Excellence"

teleconferences are available on tape and can be used for training. Consider time on e-mail and Internet use as in-house training and not playing around. I have set a personal goal to attend some sort of training each month. Even if one has a degree, continuing education is an important objective.

4. **Keep a good sense of humor.** Keep laughing at your mistakes. We all make many mistakes so instead of getting uptight remember to laugh. It relieves a lot of stress. Enjoy your job, and your mutual profession.

3. **Stress teamwork.** Teamwork is very important. Hold regularly scheduled meetings and encourage participation in organizational decisions especially when it may concern their area. Ensure all staff know the library's mission and how their job assists in meeting the library's goals.

2. **Remember what "professionalism" means.** Remember professionalism is most important and is an attitude not just a job description. Life experiences can balance the lack of formal training. Make sure they know about support associations, COLT and other paraprofessional groups or training. Encourage them to participate in local boards, councils, and associations.

1. **Practice empowerment.** Help people reach their full potential. Let staff make some decisions and have responsibilities. Encourage the paras to get involved in professional development opportunities such as ALA. Encourage your staff to consider their position as a career and not just a job. Don't be slow in granting authority and responsibility. There are lots of untapped knowledge, skills, new ideas, and valuable resources within your staff. Purchase business cards for your staff. Help them reach their full potential.

[Maxwell and Evelyn Harrell Memorial Library, Bristol, Florida. Reprinted with permission.]

Supervising Professional and Nonprofessional Staff

Listen to your employees. You need to get to know them on an individual basis. The better you know your employees the better you will be able to judge their abilities and their character. Let staff know individually that they are a part of a team and that their jobs are just as important as everyone else's whether they are professional or technical.

Praise your employees. When they go the extra mile for a patron or do an exceptional job, let them know it. They need to know that they are appreciated. Good news travels fast and they may be recruited somewhere else. Everyone wants to have a good team. Praise them among their peers and in front of patrons. Don't take these employees for granted.

Delegate. When you try to do everything yourself it makes your staff feel as though you don't think that they can handle their jobs. It makes more work for you and you will have poorly motivated employees. As you get to know your staff, you will know what qualities each person has to offer. Some are very organized, some are perfectionists, and some are procrastinators. Some staff are great with computers and others are great with children. Delegate work to those able to do the best job. If you need something typed, delegate that job to someone who can type using the computer and can save your document for you to review. That person could also type your report each month when given the information. Have one person on staff that you can trust to do your administrative duties when you are busy with other things.

Publicly apologize to your staff if you misinform them or if you think that you offended them in any way. They will see that you too are human and human beings do make mistakes.

Never downplay the importance of your staff's problems. If you see a staff member upset or crying, stop whatever you are doing and go talk to them. Ask if they would like to talk about it to you or someone else that they feel more comfortable with. Don't make a spectacle of the situation. Allow the employee time alone to talk to you or someone else in a private place. If you don't think that they can productively work the rest of the day, allow them to go home. They can make that time up later on. Some people have personal problems that are overwhelming to them and they need time to get back to normal. They are not in a position to think clearly and keeping them at work just makes the situation worse.

Never be too busy to talk to your staff. When your employees see that you are understanding and you treat them the way you would want to be treated, they will give more of themselves to their jobs. Most employees will not take advantage of that situation.

Ask for staff suggestions and use them when you can. When staff suggestions are implemented let others know, including patrons. If a patron comments about something new that they like, tell them who suggested it. It not only makes that staff member feel good, it lets patrons know that you are working as a team. I have heard great ideas and not so great ideas. Treat every idea with respect. The worst thing you can do is to make fun of someone's idea. If an idea or suggestion is presented to you that you know won't work, talk to the staff member who suggested it and together discuss the pros and cons of the idea. Usually once everything is discussed, the staff member will realize that, because of the specifics that you two talked about, the idea will not work. Tell them that you appreciated the suggestion and if they can think of anything else to make things flow more smoothly to let you know. Give every idea some thought. Don't think that just because an entry-level staff member suggested something it wouldn't work. They are usually the ones at the service desk the most and know what will make their jobs run more smoothly. If you are not sure whether an idea will work or not, try it! You may be pleasantly surprised.

Communicating with Your Staff and Others

Communication is a very important aspect of branch management. Communicating with your staff and patrons must be clear and accurate. Staff complain most when you have communicated ineffectively or not at all. They become confused and frustrated if they are not sure what you want them to do. Be clear in job descriptions that are distributed to staff. Make all library policies, grievance procedures, and telephone numbers of the administrative staff available to your employees.

Give your staff your home telephone number. Tell them to feel free to use it to call you if they are not feeling well or have a family emergency and won't be coming in to work. Do not allow your staff to call you to talk about their coworkers, however. Do not allow your staff to document each other unless it is a supervisor who is having problems with an employee. Those issues can be discussed in your office with the door closed. The intended reason for having your staff call you at home is to tell you that they won't be able to work for one reason or another. When staff call you at home, don't be annoyed. If you take the day off, would you rather get a telephone call about a situation going on at the branch that may need your attention, or an angry telephone call from your boss after the fact? Keep the lines of communication open between you and your staff.

Oral Communication

Provide proper retraining of existing staff as needed. Allow staff to communicate their ideas on decisions to be made that affect the entire branch. Communicate information received from managers meetings to your staff. Have employees communicate information from their committee and other meetings. When new technologies are added to the library system, make sure all staff know how to use them. All staff need to know what is going on at your branch, not just those staff members involved in a particular event. For example, if there is a children's program going on or coming up, all public service staff need to know about it. Patrons visit all service desks and may ask the reference librarian about children's programming.

Don't allow your oral communication to become a monologue, however. Allow the other person to communicate their thoughts and feelings. Don't argue or try to push your ideas on others. No matter how long you have been a librarian or worked in your library system, you will not be an expert on every aspect of library service. There is nothing wrong with talking things over with your staff if you are not sure about procedures that they do every day. If you disagree with something that is said by a staff member, just tell them that you don't agree. Don't make them feel bad for contributing by telling them that they are wrong. The easiest way to disrupt communication is to make employees apprehensive about speaking to you and sharing ideas. Not only will they not communicate with you, they won't listen to what you have to say.

Don't introduce staff using titles unless it is necessary for the other person to know what those titles are. When you introduce your circulation staff to someone you might say, "This is John Doe, he is a part of my circulation team." Most patrons don't care whether the person helping them has a library degree or not. They just want someone who is knowledgeable in their field and is able to provide them with the information that they need. If a patron has a specific problem and needs to speak with a supervisor, have staff introduce the supervisor to the patron as the head of that department. That way, patrons know that they are being taken care of by the supervisor. When introducing staff to your colleagues, introduce only the heads of departments as such. All others are introduced as your circulation staff, reference, or children's staff. Later on, if your colleagues want to know the levels within your branch and who occupies them, you can discuss it with them privately.

Introductions do more than tell one person who the other person is. They identify people and their place in the system. If you introduce one person as Jane Doe, LTA III, and the person standing next to her as John Doe, LTA I, John will not feel as important as Jane at that moment. You want your staff to all feel important and as an equal part of the team. You don't want any feelings of subordination on the part of any employee. Every employee knows his or her job title. It doesn't have to identify who they are as though you always want to keep each level separated and everyone in their places. I'm sure that everyone has employees in the lowest positions that are the backbones of their libraries. We could not run smoothly without them! Show them how much you appreciate them by treating them all the same and with as much respect as you give your professional librarians. Imagine your library for one day if every nonprofessional employee stayed home. We need them to feel just as important as they are to us.

Written Communication

When corresponding in writing, don't rush through and send it without looking it over. Use language that is common in the library system. Be clear and precise. If you are communicating an event, include what it is, when it is, where it is, and any additional comments. These include whether or not registration is required and the age group(s) the program is geared to.

If you send correspondence to the same outside sources frequently, have several form letters written. Ask your typist employee to type those letters into the computer, type the envelopes, show them to you for approval and signature, make copies for your files, and mail them, this employee should also be responsible for filing the computer disks and keeping them organized. Pretty soon all you would have to say is, "Please send a thank-you letter" to a certain organization. That employee would take care of everything including keeping names and addresses of community contacts in a file for easy access. Try to select one person with the best of all qualities to be your administrative assistant. Of course, you should be the only person to do all documents of a personal nature that involve any of your staff. This includes performance appraisals, documentation of staff behavior, notes from doctors about staff health, etc. Do not allow any other staff member to have access to this type of information.

Communicating with the Public—Empowering Your Staff

Allow your staff some authority when dealing with patrons. Limits on the amount of fines to waive, forgiving half of a patron's fines, believing patrons if they think they are telling the truth, and trying to satisfy the patron, are just some of the areas where staff need some authority. Allow your staff to make telephone calls to other branches to clear up discrepancies and to offer your business card to patrons who wish to speak to you. Let your staff know how you would handle a situation and how you want them to handle it in your absence. Patrons get frustrated if they are having a problem and the person helping them can't do anything about it. Don't allow your staff to break any rules or to disregard the policy, but do allow them some authority to be able to help patrons to reconcile their problems.

Just like your staff, you take days off, go to meetings, and call in sick. You can't be at the branch every minute. When you are away from your branch you shouldn't be worrying about what your staff is doing. Give your staff confidence. Sometimes when I plan to take some time off, I will openly tell everyone that I am glad that I have such a great staff that can handle the branch while I am gone. I let them know that I am confident that everything will be fine when I return. Make your staff want to come to work, not dread being there. Reassure them and let them know that you are supporting them. Don't treat them like children and assume that they can't do something. Some of your staff may be older than you are. They will resent a younger person treating them like a child.

Your staff can be a great shield between you and a patron when they have a great relationship with you. For example, when angry patrons complain about something and ask to see the manager, the staff person involved could make the situation worse by saying unkind things about you to the patron. If your staff dislikes you because you bully them or they are afraid of you, they will hand you problem patrons on a silver platter. That will be their way of getting back at you.

On the other hand, they could make the situation better by telling the patron that they would be happy to get the manager but they would also be happy to help them in any way that they can. The staff member could explain the policy to the patron and tell them what can be done within the bounds of their authority. If the patron is still not happy they can offer your business card if you are not there. If you are there, the staff member would come into your office and apprise you of the situation before you talk to the patron. Many times the patron is calmer once they have been offered alternatives by the staff person involved. I have been at the desk when patrons didn't know that I was the manager. They would have a problem and ask to see the person in charge. I witnessed the discussion between employee and patron and a potentially angry patron was calmed down and left the building happy. If your staff have good customer-service skills, you job will be much easier. After the encounter was over, I praised that employee in front of her coworkers. Other staff members that witnessed the encounter now know how to handle a similar situation. I didn't have to get involved with the patron at all.

If that same staff member were afraid of me, she would not have even attempted to handle the situation for fear of doing something wrong. She would have immediately said, "Here is our branch manager, would you like to talk to her?" You don't have to be involved in every encounter. You will be burned out and dislike your job because you are spending more time diffusing situations than you are managing your branch. My circulation person was confident even with me standing there that she was doing and saying the right things. She also knew that if she didn't handle the situation successfully she would not be yelled at or embarrassed in front of her coworkers. This is what you want to achieve with your staff. Knowledge, confidence, and experience to handle almost any situation.

Allow your employees to work. Don't look over their shoulders. No one likes to be watched while they are working. Allow your staff the space they need to do their jobs effectively. Go into your office and get your own work done. Don't stay in there all day but do allow your employees the chance to work without worrying about doing something wrong in front of the boss. When you are at a meeting or taking the day off, how does your staff perform? They know where you are if they need you. If a patron comes in and gives them problems, they will come and get you. Allow employees to attempt to solve their own problems. If someone calls in sick and the circulation desk schedule needs to be adjusted, allow your head of circulation to make the changes. When employees bring problems to you, ask them what they think should be done. As long as the situation is not an emergency, talk to your employees about ways to solve problems rather than just handing them over to you. You need to have confidence in your staff that they can solve problems competently when you are not there. Usually they know what to do; they just need confirmation from you.

You want your branch to work like a strong chain, with everyone depending on someone else. You can't afford to have gaps in communication or tasks at your branch. For example, when the library pages bring in the book return to be discharged, it shouldn't sit in the workroom until a nonprofessional can get to it. Whoever is not on the desk and is not involved in something else at the moment should work on it. From time to time every staff member, including you, should clear the books that were in the book return. No job involving books placed on a book truck should just sit and wait. This is especially true for items still attached to patron records. Reserves, books from other branches, etc., should be processed as soon as possible by an available staff member. Under no circumstances should any job wait until a staff member is back from sick leave or vacation, especially when it involves a patron. I'm not talking about one item where there is a question or problem, I am talking about situations where all patron requests are placed on a desk until that person returns.

Allow all of your employees to be exposed to the same information. Don't circulate professional journals only to librarians. How do you think the others would feel knowing that they are not "allowed" to read a library magazine? Although they work in a library and can identify with a lot of the stories in the magazine, they don't have a library degree so they are not "important enough" to read it. What about new and upcoming titles? Shouldn't every staff member be aware so that they can alert the public of new titles by their favorite authors? Many staff members may choose not to read those library magazines, but let it be their choice. The same is true for workshops. Route all information to everyone. Even if you think that a workshop may not apply to someone's job or you may assume that they are not interested, show it to them anyway. What is the harm? If they attend the workshop they can only gain knowledge and feel more a part of a team with the professional librarians.

Meetings

Have regular meetings with your staff. Meetings are a good way to make sure everyone knows the procedures and is of one accord. Announcements can be made and it gives everyone the feeling that they are in fact a team. Meetings with your staff must serve a purpose. Whether it is to inform them of new procedures, to share minutes from your branch manager meetings, or to solve a problem, you need to make sure everyone knows why they are there. Don't have a meeting just to be having one where no one has anything to say. Ask your staff what they would like to talk about.

If the agenda is distributed ahead of time, staff are more likely to contribute to the meeting because they will be more prepared. Keep the meeting positive. Don't try to cover too many topics at one meeting. Don't ever embarrass a staff member about their performance in front of the rest of the staff. Performance problems should be dealt with privately.

When you are planning meetings with staff make sure you post the meeting date and time in a prominent place. Give each staff member a copy of the agenda so that they will be ready to contribute to the meeting. On the day of the meeting, arrive a few minutes early to set up and get organized. Always begin your meeting on time. If you wait for everyone to arrive before you begin the meeting, your staff will not make an effort to be on time. Ask one of your staff to take minutes from the meeting. The minutes can be used for staff that could not attend the meeting. Bring copies of handouts for each staff member rather than passing around one copy for everyone to see. Make sure everyone has a chance to ask questions. After the meeting, thank them for coming.

Delegating

Practice effective delegation. The best way to show that you are willing to invest in your support staff and to accomplish most of the suggestions I've given is to learn how to delegate. No one likes working for bosses who can't seem to get anything done because they cannot or will not let go of tasks that someone else can do.

Delegation offers a twofold reward: It lets your staff operate more efficiently and it shows your confidence in them by allowing them the opportunity to stretch their abilities. If your staff has reached the top of their classifications, delegating new tasks to them may be their only chance for job enrichment. This is even more effective if you can provide the opportunity for them to exercise their delegation skills so they will have time to do their new tasks! There is really no other way for you to show your confidence in their abilities.

Failure to delegate seems to be the main problem librarians have with letting go of clerical or other nonprofessional tasks that the paraprofessional should be doing. But beware of two pitfalls in delegation. First, don't delegate a task to an employee who does not have the skills to handle it; this breeds failure and loss of confidence. And please don't delegate tasks everyone knows you dislike doing while you hold onto those things you enjoy doing. Your staff can tell what you're up to and instead of being encouraged by your confidence in them, they will recognize they are being dumped on.

["Managing Your Support Staff: An Insider's View" by Shirley Rais. *Whole Library Handbook 2*, by George Everhart. Reproduced with permission.]

Compensatory Time and the Book Return

Offer compensatory time to your staff, giving them opportunities to do extra work in exchange for time off You will be amazed at how much work can be accomplished when you offer this flexibility to your staff. For example, I have employees volunteering months ahead of time to empty the book return when the library is closed. Each branch is different so the amount of compensatory time offered will be different. If you have a large branch with more than one book return, of course the amount of compensatory time offered will be greater than that of a small library. Set a specific time of day that the book return must be emptied. Make sure the person has a key to the building and knows the alarm codes if applicable. The book return should be emptied and the books sorted according to the area of the collection they belong in. For example, sort all new books together on the book truck, all juvenile fiction books together, etc. When the books are brought in and discharged once the library reopens, they will be easier to sort and either shelve or place on sorting shelves.

You should offer more compensatory time than it actually takes to empty the book return to provide an incentive. If it actually takes thirty minutes to empty and sort it, offer one hour. Have a set time allowed and a schedule posted so that everyone knows who will be responsible and when. Offer an extra hour on holidays. On days when the library is closed and the book returns are emptied, staff should practice good customer service. Leave the lights off in the building if possible and the doors locked while staff are working outside. Patrons are sure to walk or drive up while someone is out there to ask questions about using the library that day. Have your staff politely tell the patron that you are closed today and let them know when you will reopen. If patrons ask to go into the library to get a book, have your staff explain that they are only there to empty the book return and that no one is allowed in the building when it is closed except for that purpose. If patrons want to return books while staff are outside, they should accept the materials from the patron, smile, and tell the patron to have a nice day. If the patron is worried about overdue charges, assure them that they can take care of it when the library opens. They will not incur any extra fees while the library is closed. Remember, anytime you or your staff are on library property, treat patrons as if it were a regular work day. Always use good customer-service skills.

Personal Time

Allow employees time off to take care of personal matters. From time to time employees will need to take some of their accrued leave time to take care of personal business. Unless your employees are willing to disclose the nature of their business, don't ask. They should feel that they can get time off without having to explain a very private matter. Your employee may be having marital problems or have a family member in trouble with the law. Unless it interferes with their job performance, it is none of your business. Don't assume that an employee is taking time off to avoid being at work.

Allow employees time off to do those things that are important to them and the community. For example, if the Red Cross is having a blood drive in your area, allow your staff to participate. Your staff needs time off to vote, to serve on juries, and to participate in reserve duty. Make sure that you stagger the times that staff leave the building but do allow them to go. If your staff feels free to work and be able to participate in other activities, they will perform better. They won't feel isolated from the world while they are at work. You don't want the workplace to be a prison. It is better to have someone take a day off occasionally than to allow stress and problems to build up so they are out for weeks.

Employees with children have specific needs for time off. They will request more personal time off for school activities, emergencies involving their children, and vacation time.

Vacation Time

Inform your staff that they must apply for vacation time in advance. Once the weekly schedule is completed, changes should be kept to a minimum. Find out what your library's policy is on leave time and how far in advance it should be requested. When holidays occur don't allow the same staff members to take extended time off each year. Allow everyone to take time off on different days so that everyone has a chance to enjoy the holidays. Don't allow staff to request vacation time months ahead of time just to jump ahead of everyone else. Make sure that forms are filled out by all employees, signed by you, and written down on a large calendar centrally located for all the staff to see. Do not accept leave forms more than a month or so in advance. No one knows what the needs of the branch will be much farther in advance. If staff have made reservations to go out of town, of course you would want to know that in advance. Leave should be granted based on staff availability and branch needs. Keep copies of leave request forms in your employee's files.

Required Time Off

Find out your library system's policy involving other types of leave such as educational leave, military leave, professional leave, and jury duty.

Military leave and jury duty are two types of leave that are required time away from the workplace. Employees who have military reserve duty or jury duty should not be punished for not being available to work. For example, if you know that someone will be gone for a week to serve on a jury, don't make them work double shifts on the service desk to try to make up for the time they will be away. Try to hire a substitute if possible or rearrange your service desk schedule. Try to see things from more than one angle. You are a supervisor but you are also an employee. Think about how you would feel if your supervisor did those things to you. Even if your supervisor is not the nicest person in the world, don't follow in his/her footsteps and take your frustrations out on your employees. Everyone is accountable to their boss for their own actions. Doing something because someone else does is not an excuse.

Read your library's policy on personal leave and vacation time. Meet with all staff and discuss these policies. Don't single out staff with or without specific needs to talk to. Everyone needs to know what the policies are. Accrued leave time that is requested in advance can usually be accommodated. Document those employees who repeatedly ask for time off at the last minute. Not every request can be accommodated even if it is requested in advance. There has to be adequate staffing at the branch each hour that the library is open. Don't allow staff with children to receive special privileges and allowances for time off. Those employees without children have just as much right to time off as those with children. Their time is just as valuable to them and there should not be a distinction between the two groups. Sometimes working parents have to make sacrifices. There has to be an equal balance between employees. All employees should request leave time far enough in advance so that the schedule can accommodate that person being gone. When a staff member requests leave at the last minute, he/she needs to understand that the needs of the branch come first.

Time for Continuing Education

Don't be afraid to allow employees to further their education. Many supervisors think that if they allow their employees time off to continue their education, these employees will leave. That may true in some cases, but some employees will leave no matter what you do. It is a mistake to hinder another person from achieving their goals. If they really want to go to school or go back to school, they will do it anyway. Would you rather have an employee who resents you because you can but won't allow them to further their education, thereby lowering their motivation to work for you, or an employee who is happy to be working while achieving their goal and bringing more experience and knowledge to their job? Your employees are sensible people. If you are a great person to work for, have the qualities of an effective supervisor, allow them to be themselves and to achieve their goals while maintaining a healthy work environment, why would they want to go anywhere else? Don't try to hold onto people by making them think that they have nowhere else to go. Make them want to stay and make others want to work for you. If your employees are happy and they talk to staff at other branches about your branch, you will have long-term employee retention, and when there are vacancies, you will have more than enough applicants to fill the positions.

Volunteer Time

Finally, support employees who volunteer to help the Friends of the Library. The Friends of the Library is a great organization that helps the library in many ways. They offer financial assistance to pay for many items that the library system may not be able to afford. When staff volunteer to help at a book sale sponsored by the Friends, it ultimately helps your library. When the Friends of the Library purchase items for your specific library, do take the time to send a thank-you letter from your branch.

How to Be a Better Boss

The following is a list of things that you can do right away to become a better boss:

1. Listen to your employees. Just telling them what to do all the time will lead to low morale and performance problems.

2. Trust your employees to do their jobs effectively.

3. Be observant of what is going on with your employees.

4. Have a sense of humor about your job. Laugh!

5. Keep an open mind. Don't make negative assumptions.

6. Learn from your mistakes. Don't repeat them.

7. Don't put off or delegate jobs that you don't enjoy doing.

8. Thank your employees for doing a good job.

9. Separate your job from other aspects of your life.

10. Pace yourself.

11. If you were wrong, say so. Don't try to be superhuman for your employees.

12. Be an advocate for your staff. If you have confidence in them, they will have confidence in themselves.

13. Don't blame your mistakes on your employees.

14. Do not allow your employees to use you as the target of their problems.

Supervisory Mistakes

The following are frequent mistakes that can potentially hurt your career

1. Yelling at your employees and saying unkind things to them.

2. Not telling your boss about important incidents that happened at your branch.

3. Doing things to make your boss look bad.

4. Being absent from work excessively.

5. Setting a bad example for your employees.

6. Avoiding problem employees.

7. Having your employees supervise each other without guidance.

8. Being too hard on your employees.

9. Not understanding that employees are individuals.

To put these another way, according to Mark Eppler's *Management Mess Ups: 57 Pitfalls You Can Avoid,* here are some of the critical mistakes that managers can make.

1. Believing leadership is power instead of influence.

2. Failure to understand that the true objective of a manager is to create stars, not to be one.

3. Failure to understand that the most powerful and persuasive thing a manager can do is to listen.

4. Failure to recognize that in managing people, one size does not fit all.

5. Failure to understand that motivation is an inner drive, not something we can do to one another.

6. Failure to solicit input from employees before making changes that affect their responsibilities.

7. Failure to conduct frequent self-appraisals and make the needed adjustments.

8. Failure to understand that people will quit planting seeds if they cannot participate in the harvest.

9. Failure to understand the importance of a performance appraisal.

10. Failure to recognize the penny-wise-and-pound-foolish nature of micromanagement.

11. Failure to recognize the dangers of cynicism.

12. Failure to deserve the victory you seek. [p. 241.]

Being a boss does not mean that you have to be a dictator and exalt your authority. Everyone knows that you are the boss. Being negative towards staff, having a know-it-all attitude, and micromanaging all just show your staff how little you actually know about being a leader. Don't be unprofessional. Denying your staff promotions or raises that they deserve just because of petty instances is very unprofessional. For example, if you are carrying something heavy and a staff member does not hold the door open for you, that is not a reason to deny them a promotion. You may have been frustrated at the time but the incident had nothing to do with their work performance. Most staff accomplish a lot of work. Your lower-level staff are the backbone of your branch because they are the ones on the front lines every day. Let them know that they are appreciated.

8

Managing Your Staff, Part 1: Getting to Know Them

Care about your staff and their feelings. They are all individuals with separate lives and personalities. Take time to talk with each staff member individually. Let them know that your door is always open and that they can talk to you at any time. If you have a staff member who is usually very talkative and one day he is very quiet, ask him if he is okay. He may not tell you what's wrong but knowing that you care means a lot.

Sharing Responsibilities

Many staff have no idea how much work is involved in managing a branch. I have heard comments about other branch managers like "He doesn't do anything all day," or "I wish I had that easy job." Allow staff to be in charge of special projects. By the time the project has been planned, organized, and executed, they will see how much work is involved. Ask your staff how they would handle certain situations. Everyone from your branch assistant to your library pages has something to contribute and may suggest ways to improve their jobs that you may not have thought of.

Allow your staff to do their jobs. If they are responsible for supervising the library pages, when there is a vacancy allow them to select applications, interview, and hire whoever they think will work well for them. This gives them more responsibility and allows them to take charge of the job that they are being paid to do. Of course you will sit in on all interviews, but allow your staff to be in the forefront of conducting the interviews. They will gain experience, feel more valuable to the library, and will take their jobs more seriously.

Socializing with Your Staff

Allow your staff to socialize with you and with each other. The more at ease they feel with you the more likely they are to be motivated to come to you with problems or questions. Maintain a professional atmosphere but don't insist that the workroom be silent. People need to interact with each other to develop healthy working relationships. It is a good idea to have social events at your branch periodically so that staff get a chance to have fun with each other and socialize.

Celebrating birthdays and special events is one way to get people together. At our branch we have a luncheon once a month to celebrate staff birthdays. We post a sign on the break room door and everyone indicates what food item they would like to bring. The people who celebrated birthdays the previous month are responsible for the cake and birthday cards for those celebrating this month. This is so that each person purchases one cake per year. We all bring various dishes and socialize with each other in the break room. We put everything on the table at noon and those that are not working on the service desk at that time sing "Happy Birthday" to those celebrating. The people on the service desk share in the festivities as soon as their desk time is over. It is a nice event because there is delicious food and good conversation. You can have themes each month if you like. We have had salad luncheons, with different kinds of salads, and a pizza luncheon. Ask your staff for suggestions.

There is a pleasant area in the back of our library building that contains our staff parking lot, delivery area, and trees. During the summer we have barbecues there instead of luncheons inside. Someone brings a grill and we cook outside and enjoy the sunshine. We look forward to those luncheons because they give us a chance to unwind during our busy days. It is never mandatory and staff who do not celebrate events do not have to participate. Many staff have tried out new recipes with much success. We make sure that everyone who wants to participate has something to eat, and that there are vegetarian dishes, ethnic dishes, and so on.

In December we exchange names and buy small gifts for each other, spending $10 or less. We keep our names a secret (most of us!) and exchange gifts at our December luncheon. As the branch manager, I try to give each member of my staff a small gift to show my appreciation for their hard work and dedication during the year. A Christmas ornament, some baked goods, or just a bag of Christmas treats will show that you care.

The Break Room

If your branch has a break room, it's a good place for your staff to have lunch, chat, take a nap, or just meditate for a few minutes. Everyone needs some down time to unwind. If you have a large room it can be made more comfortable by the addition of a sofa or some other comfortable seating. A refrigerator, microwave, and drink and snack machines at the branch are very convenient. Staff may bring their lunch and eat it right at the branch.

Favorites

Don't have favorite staff members. Don't socialize after work or go to lunch with the same staff member(s) all of the time. If you are invited to lunch, go with whoever asks you. Don't just go with department heads or supervisors at your branch. You will alienate other staff and make them feel they are not as important as your higher level staff.

Always be fair. Treat all staff with the same respect that you want from them. Be consistent. Let them know what to expect from you all of the time, not just depending on your mood.

Hiring Staff

When you read job applications you will find some that seem to reflect the perfect employee. They have all of the skills, experience, and education required. They have great references and you think that you have found the person you were looking for. Don't underestimate the importance of the interview; it is your chance to test the validity of the statements made in the application. In many instances candidates exaggerate their skills in hopes of getting hired. Look over each application and write down questions that you want to ask. During the interview, don't ask the standard questions that the candidates will be expecting. Ask questions about hypothetical situations. For example, ask them how they would handle a patron who was upset about a fine incurred that they claimed they did not owe. That way, you will get an idea of their skills and personalities. Hire the person you think has the qualities you are looking for and would be the best fit with the rest of your staff. Keep one or two other choices in mind in case your first choice turns the job down or doesn't meet your expectations.

New-Employee Orientation

When you hire a new employee, make sure that she is fully trained and knows all of your policies before being left alone to work at the service desk. Have new employees visit the main library to see what the differences are between the branches and main. Explain the library's organization chart and tell them whom to call for various types of information. Allow them to work different shifts to get experience in different situations—how to work the service desk when a group is visiting, for example, and how to work when patrons have problems with their library records.

When a new employee begins work, have everything ready for the first day. You should already have a desk or another area cleared and a place to store personal belongings. All of your current staff should know the new employee's start date so there are no surprises. When the new person arrives, make her feel welcome and introduce her to the rest of the staff. Give her time to adjust to the new surroundings. Have copies of the library's policies available for her to begin reading during off-desk time. Make sure you have her paired up with one person who is in charge of training. If possible, don't let the employee doing the training be one of the candidates who also applied for the new position. There might be some hurt feelings and you don't want them reflected on the new employee.

Training Checklists

Have a training checklist ready for the new employee to see what to learn. Have each task listed separately so that nothing is forgotten. After the new employee is fully trained in a task, place a check mark, trainer's initials, and the date the task was mastered on the form.

An example of training checklist:

TASK	DONE	DATE	STAFF	COMMENTS
STAMP CARDS				
CHECK OUT ITEMS				
CLEAR FINES				
LIBRARY CARD REGISTRATION				

Of course the tasks listed on the checklist will depend upon the job. A reference librarian's checklist will be different from a circulation assistant's checklist. Develop your own checklists for every position and keep them on hand so that when new staff are hired you have the checklists ready. File the completed checklist in each new employee's folder after training and keep the lists in your file cabinet.

Here is a list of things for *you* to do when introducing new employees to your branch.

1. Provide an orientation packet.

2. Provide a name tag and business cards.

3. Discuss parking information.

4. Give a tour of your library focusing on restrooms, lounge, and location of supplies, photocopy machines, and telephones.

5. Discuss safety and security issues.

6. Discuss hours, breaks, payday, and procedures for reporting absences.

7. Discuss standards of conduct and any formal or informal dress code.

8. Make sure all personnel paperwork is completed.

9. Discuss telephone procedures and policies.

10. Explain timekeeping procedures, including overtime and compensatory time.

11. Explain benefits. (Your human resource department will probably take care of this.)

12. Explain procedures for communicating problems or concerns.

13. Discuss any probationary period.

14. Discuss performance standards and appraisal.

15. Cover grievance procedures.

16. Discuss opportunities for advancement.

["Orienting New Employees" by Katherine Branch. *Whole Library Handbook 2*, by George Eberhart. Reproduced with permission.]

Department Managers

Make sure that your department managers are trained in supervising staff. Your managers are there to make your job easier. Staff report directly to them to solve problems and be informed of procedures. Your managers should attend all library-system-wide meetings pertaining to their departments. Your circulation manager should attend meetings with circulation managers from other branches. You should meet regularly with each department manager to talk about procedures, staff, and problems. Keep the lines of communication open between you and your managers. If you have a good relationship with them and they are good supervisors who are competent in their duties, they will handle most of the day-to-day problems that occur. You should only be involved in problems that they can't handle. If all of your staff are coming directly to you with problems and questions about routine procedures, the department managers need to be more active in their roles. They need to take control of their departments and make sure that their staffs are fully trained.

Assistant Branch Manager

Train your assistant to perform your duties in your absence. You never know when you will have to be out on extended sick leave, for example, and he will have to perform those duties. Train him on how to complete all reports on the dates that they are due. Provide guidance in the decision making until you are comfortable that his decisions are the best ones for the branch. Review reports before they are submitted to another location. Make sure these reports are error-free, professional, and finished before the deadline. On the other hand, make sure you know how to do his duties as well. You two are the branch manager and acting branch manager. You should both be able to actively perform each other's duties.

Night Staff

Make sure that staff who work at night are fully trained. Schedule enough staff members to adequately provide service to all desks. Always have one person in charge of the building each night to handle patron problems and for staff to go to with procedural questions. Many patrons come in only at night because they work during the day. Students come in the evening to work on research papers and projects. Those patrons that come in the evening deserve the same high level of customer service that the patrons who visit during the day receive. You need to feel comfortable that the night staff is competent to handle any situation that arises. Leave a stack of your business cards available for staff to give to patrons who have problems and want to speak with you about them.

Library Pages

Library pages are very important members of your team. Their job is to make sure that the collection is in shelf-list order and has a pleasing appearance. Upon hiring new pages, let them know immediately what their responsibilities are. If you have a library page handbook, make sure that they read and understand it. If you don't have one, create one. It should include the library page job description, dress code, leave request procedures, who to call if they won't be coming to work, and any information they need to know in order to do their jobs effectively. In their first few weeks of employment, have them place colored paper strips in the books that they shelve. These strips should be long enough to stick out over the top of each book. Assign a staff member to supervise them and to check those books that they shelve for accuracy. Any titles that are shelved incorrectly can be flagged and the page involved can be retrained. If you hire more than one page at the same time, they should use different-colored strips. When you are confident that they are shelving accurately, the strips can be discontinued.

Talk to your library pages about good customer service. They are out on the floor and many times patrons will ask them questions. It is appropriate for them to help patrons to locate specific books. The pages should check the shelves, sorting areas, and book carts. If the item is not found, they should politely refer the patron to the information desk or to another staff member. The pages need to know that they are representing the library and they should practice good customer service whenever they are in contact with patrons.

Do not allow your library pages to wear beepers and cellular telephones while they are working. It is very distracting for them and other patrons. Keep the lines of communication open between you and your pages. Know what their relationship is with each other. (Once, two of my male pages almost had a fistfight in the stacks in front of patrons. Needless to say, they were both fired on the spot.) Have regular library page meetings. Discuss their progress, problems, and answer any questions they might have.

Hiring Library Pages

How do you find good library page candidates? Obviously there is no one correct answer. Each library is constrained by a separate set of circumstances. Some libraries can pay only minimum wage while others offer more competitive pay. Obviously the wage will have a large impact on your ability to attract candidates. Other factors which may limit the pool of prospective page candidates include the fact that other employers can offer benefits like transportation or discounts. By its nature, the job is usually less than exciting, and some libraries are limited by in-house hiring policies such as age limits and lack of opportunity for advancement.

Since salaries are usually the most difficult to address, there are other ways by which libraries can attract good candidates. Generally speaking, if the work environment is positive, people will notice. It is incumbent upon supervisors to treat their page staff with respect. You must reward initiative and responsibility. And most of all, you must establish mutual trust. Communication is the key. Make the staff aware of the hard work the pages do and the value of tasks such as properly maintaining the shelves. Let the pages know how important you think their role is. If the page staff likes working at your library it will show. If prospective employees see your staff enjoying themselves, they will want to be a part of the team.

Another important factor to consider when hiring library pages is that sometimes "the best and the brightest" students don't make the best pages. When looking at candidates, supervisors should strongly consider maturity, responsibility, and personal recommendations.

In the area of training, it is important to remember that the most important aspect of any training program is open communication. Supervisors must make themselves readily accessible. Many libraries rely on manuals to train new pages. It has been my experience that while page manuals and memos are important as points of reference, the most effective technique for training is person-to-person. Some suggestions to improve training programs include the following:

1. Using peers to conduct the majority of the training.
2. Follow up on a regular basis during the first three months.
3. Make sure the page understands that they *must* ask questions.
4. Let them make mistakes, and make sure they also correct them.

If communication is open, your chances of developing effective workers are greatly enhanced.

Evaluating Library Pages

One of the most dreaded aspects of page supervision would have to be evaluation. The supervisor's degree of dread will depend on his or her perception of evaluation. If the supervisor truly believes the evaluation process will lead to improvement rather than reviewing it as an opportunity to discipline, then the process will be more likely to succeed.

Obviously, the supervisor can't be there all the time, so the more information you can gather the better. It is critical to get as much input as possible from the rest of the staff. Librarians working at the desk must be actively involved and think of themselves as de facto supervisors when you're not around. The page/clerical staff must be working within a team mentality so that gentle correction won't be considered an affront, but rather an effort to make everyone look good.

Trust is the most important element when involving the staff in the evaluation process. The supervisor must be willing to seriously consider the input of coworkers and make sure that confidentiality is the top priority. It is important to focus on areas of strength and weakness rather than on personalities.

While it is important to consider the input of coworkers, the supervisor is ultimately responsible for the final evaluation. If the supervisor is able to convey to the staff that the purpose of the evaluation is positive, meant to improve skills rather than build up evidence to discipline or terminate employment, then the experience will more likely be a smooth and productive one.

Providing Incentives

The last and perhaps the most important area of page supervision is the area of incentives. A salary is not the only factor in being able to keep these employees happy. Providing rewards, opportunities for creative expression, and an active role in determining day-to-day tasks go a long way towards improving employee job satisfaction.

A good supervisor will find the strengths and special talents of the staff and provide the opportunities for these skills to be put to use for the benefit of the library. Giving pages opportunities for direct input in formulating procedures or devising supervision schemes, and greater responsibility in areas such as programming are ways to make the job more interesting and thereby encourage pages to continue to work hard and contribute to the team effort.

It is important to remember that, in most instances, the pay pages receive is too low for the amount of work they are required to perform. As branch manager, you are their advocate. It is your responsibility to continue to fight for higher pay and more benefits. Since pay is often one of the elements the supervisor realistically has little or no control over, it is incumbent upon the supervisor to develop a mutually satisfying relationship with their page staff, one that fosters

1. Responsibility

2. Respect

3. Trust

If your page supervisors consistently reward initiative, communicate to other staff the value of the job pages do, and always fight for more money/benefits, the pages will know they are concerned and will respect them for it.

9

Managing Your Staff, Part 2: Day-to-Day Operations

When your branch library is fully staffed and running, one of your primary tasks will be to make sure it runs smoothly. Besides the patron-related problems and challenges you and your staff will confront every day, you will have to deal with many others that relate to members of your staff themselves.

Motivation

There is no single solution to motivating any employee. No matter how hard you try, you cannot force someone to be motivated. Each person is different. Negative performance evaluations, harsh verbal criticism, or simply ignoring them will not make someone whip into shape and be a motivated employee. Doing those things will have the opposite effect, in fact. If someone is not motivated and you offer no encouragement or praise for anything they do correctly, where is the motivation? If your employees are afraid of being criticized when they do something wrong, they will not even attempt to do anything new for fear of making a mistake and being criticized even further.

How can you tell if employees are motivated? They will be happy, energetic, and ready for the next task. They will ask to try new things, learn new skills, and help others with their tasks. Motivated staff members are not upset by change and they try to make the rest of the team feel good about themselves and the job. Employees who are not motivated don't care about their jobs. They do not volunteer to help with projects or serve on committees. These staff members are usually sad or in a bad mood. They often ask for a lot of days off and leave early on a regular basis. They resist change and complain about everything.

Some employees will not be motivated no matter what you do or say. Getting staff involved in decision making on important projects makes them feel needed. When they feel their jobs don't matter, they become complacent and unmotivated. You can't afford to have staff that don't care about their jobs. That attitude will usually carry over to the service desk and their customer-service will suffer.

There are some things that you as a manager can do to raise the level of motivation in your staff. First of all, have a talk with each of them and ask questions about their job. Are they happy? Do they feel needed? Do they feel that what they do is important to your branch and to the library system? What changes would make them feel better? The answers to these questions will give you an idea of how they are feeling.

If some employees feel their work is unimportant, give them a project to work on. One example would be programming; let employees plan and advertise a program. A successful program will boost confidence levels and perhaps motivate them to try other things. Take it slowly. If you have an employee that you want to keep on staff but would like to be more motivated, it will be worth your time to work individually with that person. Remember that every employee is different. Get to know them individually and you will be in a better position to see what motivates each of them. One person might be motivated simply by being told, "Good job!" Look at everyone's job description. Are you matching the skills with staff abilities? Don't ask someone to be in charge of creating new forms using the computer unless you are sure they have been fully trained and are capable of performing that task.

Staff Morale

There are many reasons for low morale in any work place. The biggest reason, however, is micromanagement. You might think that being involved in every aspect of your staff's job is the way to supervise them, but it is a big mistake. First of all, it tells them that you don't have confidence in their abilities and you don't trust them enough to do a good job. I have seen many supervisors try to control their staffs' jobs and actions. When staff become unmotivated and resign, such a supervisor usually has no idea why. In many instances the supervisor does not even know how to do the job; they give orders and make changes without consulting those involved. I have heard managers say, "I have been a librarian for 20 years, I know better than any staff member." If the staff who work the circulation desk every day have been working for several years, shouldn't they be consulted on circulation matters? Many managers who have not worked the circulation desk for 20 years or more will make decisions for people who work the desk every day. It does not make you any less a manager to talk to your subordinates before making decisions that affect them. You will be more respected for valuing their opinion. Make sure that you can perform every job that you are supervising. If a patron calls you to complain about their borrower's record, you should be able to search their record in the computer, interpret whatever the problem is, state the library's policy, and offer a solution to the problem. Don't be in the position of having to call the patron back because you don't understand the circulation procedures and need to ask someone else. Staff quickly lose respect for a boss who tries to supervise something he or she knows very little about.

Avoid always being negative towards staff. Negativity has never been a motivator and it never will be. You can tell an employee what to do but you can't make him want to do it. When someone wants to do something, he will do his best and want to please you. If all of the feedback that your employees receive is negative, they will give up trying to please you and either find another job or do the bare minimum to keep their current jobs.

Nip problems in the bud. If there are problems between staff members, give them a chance to work them out. If a problem interferes with their job performance or if the atmosphere becomes tense, talk to each staff member alone. After getting both sides of the story, talk to them together and try to resolve the situation. If it is a personality conflict, let them know that they must have a working relationship. They don't have to be friends off the job but they must be able to communicate at the service desk in a professional manner. Under no circumstances should an argument ensue between two staff members at the service desk.

Staff You Dislike

It is just human nature that there will be people that you dislike. One such may be a member of your staff. If this happens, try to figure out what it is that you don't like. If it is behavior or performance, talk about it together and try to push for more professionalism. If it is a personality conflict that does not affect job performance or ability to get along with everyone else, don't worry about it. Don't tell anyone your feelings or treat that staff member any differently. Try to focus on performance rather than personality. If this individual has a bad attitude and does not get along with the rest of the staff, have a talk together and discuss why the bad attitude must change if the employee wants to continue to be a part of your team. Tell this person that you have received complaints from the rest of the staff about their attitude. Do not tell the individual or anyone else about your personal dislikes—it can really come back to haunt you later. This person could apply for a promotion and be turned down because of performance but think that it is because of your personal opinion. Such an individual may even file a grievance against you. Remember that the larger your staff, the more varied the personalities. Everyone is different, but all should believe that their boss feels the same about them all.

Staff Who Complain

Ask to have a meeting with employees who complain. Don't allow them to continuously grumble aloud to everyone. Ask them what the problems are and offer to help. Tell them that their constant complaining is making others complain and it is not good for morale. Ask them to come and talk to you whenever they feel like airing their grievances. During your meeting, ask them what changes they would make to improve their jobs. Are they willing to go back to school for more training, or attend additional workshops? Asking for solutions to complaints may prevent employees from making so many complaints about their job. Don't ignore staff that complain; it only makes them complain more.

Discrimination

You must not tolerate discrimination against patrons, staff or colleagues. Do not allow your staff to place patrons in generalized categories based on race, age, gender, sexual identity, or handicap. You must not discriminate against people of any race, creed, or religion. Everyone should be treated as individuals. Sometimes it is hard to treat every patron the same way. When a patron has been rude to you in the past and wants you to help them find the information that they need, you may be tempted to give less than quality service to that patron. Don't do it! You are a professional. Do not allow anyone to lower your standard of service.

If you have a staff member who is prejudiced against another staff member or a certain group of patrons, this is a serious situation. Remember that all staff represent your branch. You must have a staff whose members are able to work together, be there to help each other, and to give all patrons the best possible service. You will need to decide how important this person is to your library. Being unable to be objective towards the rest of the staff and towards patrons, this person will alienate your staff and cause resentment and dissension. Each person has to be able to keep their opinions to themselves and be a team player. If they can't, they are not fulfilling the goals of your branch or the library system. Their job performance will suffer because they are not giving the best service to each patron. Your branch's reputation is based on how the public percieves the library and its employees. Don't put yourself in a situation where a patron accuses you of having a branch that allows discrimination.

Problem Employees

When you realize that you have a problem employee, take care of the situation as soon as possible. If you put it off the problem will only get worse. Schedule a meeting with the employee as soon as possible. Prepare your comments ahead of time so that you won't forget the key points that you want to talk about. Include an opening about why you are meeting with this employee, what the problem areas are, and how and when you expect improvement. If possible, write a list of problem areas with possible solutions to give to the employee. Have the meeting in the morning before you have to deal with other stressors of the day. Have a positive attitude and be prepared to listen. Your employee will be defensive and give reasons for actions and behavior. Make notes about the concerns so they can be documented after the meeting is over. Be honest with your employee about what concerns you. Remain calm and keep an even tone throughout the meeting.

Have examples of the problem behavior noted so when the employee asks (and they will) you will be ready. For example, if you accuse them of always arriving late for work, make sure you have the documentation to prove it. Have the day, date, and time arrived. For every problem area, make sure you have the appropriate documentation. Do not ask other staff to come in and verify your information. You don't want to alienate staff from each other. Don't be vague in your criticisms. Just saying that they have a habit of being late will cause the employee to say something like "I have only been late once. When have I been late any other time?" If you keep good records, the employee will have no reason to dispute your complaints. Unless it is an emergency, try not to meet with an employee without being prepared. Do your homework. The better prepared you are, the more smoothly the meeting will go. Employees generally get upset because they feel they are being accused of something when there is no proof to back it up. They feel that they are great employees, but their supervisor does not like them and is picking on them for no reason. You should have enough documentation that they don't have any grounds for a grievance.

At the end of the meeting, tell the employee what changes need to be made in what specific time period to improve job performance. If you have already had an initial meeting with the employee, or have given verbal and written warnings, and the behavior or performance has not improved, follow the guidelines of your library system's disciplinary policy. Keep in constant communication with your supervisor and the human resources manager. During the disciplinary process it is very important that everything be documented. If an employee is terminated and they feel they were treated unfairly, you and the library could be faced with a lawsuit. Keep accurate records and send copies to the human resources department each time you have a meeting with the employee or an incident with them needs to be documented. Make sure that you include the name of the employee, the date, the time, and the entire incident. It is also a good idea to document each meeting. Type up a report and have everyone involved sign it as verification of the specifics of the meeting. All of these documents will be very helpful if you need proof of the disciplinary process and an accurate description of what was said. If an employee must be fired, you should both go to Human Resources. It should not be done at your branch, where the employee could cause a scene. Don't worry about the other employees at your branch. They are probably glad that person is gone. Other employees who have performance problems may improve if they see that you are willing to fire anyone who is not doing their job.

Reprimands

When a staff member uses bad judgment when handling a situation, take her aside and explain the proper procedure or correct behavior. Never reprimand an employee in front of their coworkers or a patron.

Absenteeism

Getting to know your employees individually is the only way you will feel comfortable about believing them when they call in sick. If you have an employee who comes to work every day and does a great job, you would expect that if they call in sick they must really be sick. Most dedicated employees will come in to work not feeling well just to finish that project or because they know that the branch is short staffed. You don't want to condone sick employees coming in to work, because they may infect others, but it is admirable that they are that dedicated. Those employees who abuse sick leave are easy to recognize. They complain about their job and how little it pays. They are not motivated and are the first ones out of the door at the end of the day. They call in sick on Mondays and Fridays and are vague about their illnesses. They often have others call in sick for them. If you have an employee whom you suspect of abusing their sick leave, document each time they call in. Be sure to include the day of the week, the time they call, whether that day is a paid holiday when the library is open, or if some special event is going on in the community and the employee has run out of accrued leave. Keep your information in a file so that you have it available if you need to talk to them about it. Give all of your employees a specific procedure for calling in sick. Employees themselves should call, by a certain time in the morning, and they must speak with a supervisor. They shouldn't call and speak with one of their coworkers and tell that person to tell you that they won't be in. If they are out of work longer than the time limit set by your system, they should bring in a doctor's note.

Theft

If you or any one of your staff suspects that someone at the branch is stealing, this must be dealt with immediately. This situation is one that you should handle yourself; do not ask a staff member to spy on one of their coworkers. It causes dissension within your staff and you have to be absolutely certain that the accusation is true. Sometimes there are staff conflicts and accusations are made that are not true. Also, the staff member accused must be presumed innocent until you have proof of their guilt. Talk to the accuser. Get details about their knowledge of the situation. Ask them why they suspect that staff person and what proof they have. Tell them that you will take care of it and thank them for coming in to talk to you. Do not continue to inform the accusing staff member of your plans or observations. Talk to your supervisor about the accusation and decide with him or her how it should be handled. Observe the accused discreetly and document your findings. If you suspect money is taken from the cash register in the evenings, come in early in the morning and count the money. Compare the total in the safe to the total amount taken in on the cash register receipt. Also, have staff write their initials on the tape every time the No Sale key is pressed. If they are giving change for a bill and ring the No Sale key, they will be responsible for reporting that transaction to their supervisor. Just because the cash register totals don't match the actual money in the drawer, don't assume that someone is stealing. Accidents happen all the time and a person ringing in $10.00 when the actual fine is $.10 will make the day's receipts appear to be short $9.90. Make absolutely sure that there is a basis for any inquiry into whether or not any of your staff is stealing.

Make sure everyone's handbags and valuables are locked at all times. If there is no way be sure who is stealing, have a meeting with the entire staff to discuss the recent theft at the branch. Tell everyone to make sure his or her valuables are secure at all times. Many people have access to the workroom—delivery people, volunteers, lost patrons, friends of staff members, etc. Tell everyone to keep the back door locked, and not to leave non-staff people in the workroom alone. If you witness a staff member stealing they should be fired immediately. Find out from the administration if charges are to be filed.

Romance Between Staff Members

If you suspect or know for sure that two of your staff members are romantically involved, you have a choice about how to handle it. If the relationship is not affecting their work performance and they are not showing visible signs of affection in the public area, ignore it. On the other hand, neither of them should be in a position to promote or evaluate the other. If inappropriate behavior is being displayed, you should have a talk with them together and tell them your concerns. The workroom is not a place for nonprofessional behavior. Every staff member should behave appropriately for a professional organization at all times.

Sexual Harassment

Talk to the human resources department and find out your library's policy on sexual harassment. Talk to your staff about sexual harassment and what actions constitute harassment. Let your staff know that sexual harassment in any form will not be tolerated. If you overhear a conversation that can be considered sexual harassment, stop the conversation immediately. If your staff know that such conversations and actions will not be tolerated, they are less likely to engage in them. If your employees are not sure what constitutes sexual harassment, have examples ready for them. Some examples are telling someone how nice they look in tight clothing, touching someone inappropriately, or telling someone that it would be to their advantage on the job if they would be more than friends with them. Anytime staff feel uncomfortable about a comment or conversation, it is probably sexual harassment. Let your staff know that if they say to others something they would not want said to one of their relatives, it may be considered to be sexual harassment. "If one of your staff claims to have been sexually harassed, take care of the situation immediately. Never allow harassment to continue without it being addressed."

(*Sexual Harassment Manual for Managers and Supervisors: How to Prevent and Resolve Sexual Harassment Complaints in the Workplace*, by Paul Gibson. Reproduced with permission.)

Personal Telephone Calls

Decide how you want to handle personal telephone calls for staff at work; it may not be a problem at your branch. If personal telephone calls become frequent, however, or last more than a few minutes, or are taken at the service desk, you need to speak to your staff. If one staff member is abusing the telephone by accepting and placing numerous personal telephone calls, speak to that staff member. If more than one person is abusing the telephone, have a meeting and let everyone know what your policy is. It is not realistic to prohibit staff from receiving personal telephone calls; their spouses, children, and other family members will need to get in touch with them. You yourself will have personal telephone calls that you need to take. You shouldn't accept personal telephone calls but then prevent your staff from accepting them. If personal telephone calls get to be a problem, let your staff know what your policy is. It should include the following:

1. No personal telephone calls accepted or placed at the service desk.
2. Limit the amount of time a person should spend on a personal telephone call.
3. Limit the frequency of telephone calls placed.

Every time a staff member uses the telephone for a personal call, one of your telephone lines is unavailable to patrons to call in for library service.

Signing In and Out

Create a sign-in sheet for you and your staff. Place it near the door used most frequently by your staff probably in the workroom area. List the names of all staff alphabetically with columns for signing their time in and out. When they arrive for work, they should sign their time in. If they go to lunch or leave the building for any reason, they should sign out. When they return they need to sign in again.

There are many reasons that the sign-in sheet is a good idea. First of all, if you have one for each day it can be referred to when it is time to complete the payroll sheets. Second, it will alert you to any schedule changes, people leaving early, coming in later, etc. Also, if someone receives a telephone call, you can check the sheet to see whether or not you should look around the building for them. You can also purchase a sign-in board but most of these do not include the times. If someone has an hour for lunch and they sign out at noon, you should expect them to return about 1:00. If staff leave early unexpectedly, you know how many hours should be recorded for sick or annual leave.

The Kitty

To prevent having to always ask staff to donate money to buy get well cards, wedding gifts or baby gifts for staff, you may want to think about having a kitty or staff petty-cash fund. Each person could pay about $1 per month each month or pay $12 at once for the year. One person keeps track of who paid and how much. The money should be kept at the branch, locked in the safe or wherever you place your fines taken each day. When events arise such as a member of the staff being hospitalized, money from the kitty can be used to pay for cards or flowers. With a kitty arrangement, staff don't have to feel bad about being asked to donate money when they may be low on funds. When they have extra money they can pay the kitty.

10

Managing Your Staff, Part 3: Performance and Other Matters

Staff Performance

Have clear guidelines for your staff's job performance. Let them know what you expect from them and what is unacceptable. Make sure that every staff member has a copy of his or her job description. Don't assume that they know exactly what their responsibilities are.

Performance Appraisals

If you are new in your job, don't read past employee performance appraisals as a way to get to know your staff. Develop your own opinions about their performance and work habits. You don't want to cloud your thoughts with someone else's opinions that may be off base. When it is time to evaluate your staff, record your thoughts and then see how your evaluation compares with previous appraisals. Document anything that you would like to add to your employee's performance appraisals during the year. Let your staff know that you will be keeping track of their accomplishments. If they planned and executed a successful program, tell them that you will add that information to their file for appraisal. By the same token, make notes about their performance that include excessive sick leave taken, tardiness, and customer-service problems. Try to begin and end every performance appraisal meeting on a positive note. Don't discuss staff members' personal lives or job performance with other staff, for obvious reasons.

Effective Performance Appraisals: Tips for Supervisors

CONDUCTING THE APPRAISAL

When conducting an appraisal, let your employee begin talking. Listen without interruption and take notes. Repeat back to your employee what they said as you understood it. Ask your employee what he or she thinks should be done to resolve problems. Talk about what should be done and what goals will be set. Don't dwell on what happened in the past. Don't allow the appraisal to be a totally negative document. Emphasize strengths and improvements made since the last appraisal. Be prepared to discuss why you rated the employee the way you did. They will ask for examples of problems stated as well as dates when they occurred.

HANDLING EMPLOYEE BEHAVIORS

If the employee becomes defensive, just listen to everything he or she has to say. Don't get into an argument with the employee. Don't lose your temper and say negative or unkind things about the employee. Maintain eye contact and ask open-ended questions. If the employee is unresponsive, be patient and ask him or her what should be done to resolve the problems. Tell the employee that you are interested in how they feel and what they have to say.

CLOSING AND FOLLOW-UP

Summarize the entire appraisal and ask the employee if there is anything else that he or she would like to discuss. Both you and the employee must sign the appraisal. Signing the appraisal does not mean that the employee agrees with everything written, it means that they have seen it and had an opportunity to discuss it. If the employee wants to write a response, allow him or her to do so and attach it to the appraisal. Provide the employee with a copy of their appraisal. End on a positive note.

Promotions

Whenever a position becomes vacant, those staff members who are in lower positions will begin to make plans to apply for the possible promotion. It is difficult to fill a position when more than one person is qualified and they already work at your branch. Sometimes even outside candidates are just as qualified as your staff. Everyone on staff that is qualified should be interviewed. Make sure that the candidate you select is the candidate best suited for the job. Just because someone has worked for the branch for several years does not mean that they should have an automatic promotion. Sometimes feelings are hurt after promotions, but if you talk to staff individually about why they were not promoted, they usually understand why the decision was made to extend the offer to another candidate. Tell them what changes they need to make in their performance or behavior to make themselves more viable candidates for the next promotional opportunity.

Promoting from Within

You might have viable candidates for your vacancy right at your branch. There may be a staff member who already knows how to do the job and is deserving of a promotion. There are obvious advantages to promoting such a person: you already know their strengths, weaknesses, personality, and work habits. Promoting from within shows your staff that if they work hard, they, too, can be promoted. The main disadvantage of promoting from within is that there may be more than one candidate at your branch that can fill the position. Hiring one staff member could well cause resentment in the person who did not receive the promotion. Also, if the person promoted fails at his new position, he may not be able to return to his previous position. Although you might be tempted to always hire from within, remember that a new person will bring in new ideas and new perspectives on things. It is good to have a balance between current and new staff.

Sharing Desks

When your staff is large and the workroom is small, people may have to share desk space. At our location only branch and department managers have their own desks. Everyone else shares a desk with another staff member. When staff need to share desks, you need to consider doing the following:

- Stagger their desk time so that they are not both trying to sit at the desk at the same time.
- Pair people who have similar interests and get along well.
- Part-time staff may not need a desk. If their job is primarily working the service desk, just make sure they have a place to put their personal items.
- Allow each person access to all drawers and files in the desks they share; don't allow one staff member to lock a drawer if they are sharing a desk with someone else. If they want to lock their handbags in the drawer, put both handbags in the same drawer and give them both a key. Staff are less likely to steal if they know they would be the obvious accused person.

Second Jobs

Many of your staff will be employed by other organizations. When I interview people for positions within the branch, I ask each applicant if they have any problems working the schedule of the job for which they are applying. I also ask if a change to work schedule here would make a problem for them. Applicants with other jobs will talk about any conflicts that might arise. There is nothing wrong with hiring an applicant with another job. Make sure that the hours when you need them are not conflicting with their other job. Make it clear that you cannot adjust your schedules to accommodate their other schedule. Your job needs to be their primary one. You do not want to be in a position where every week you have to change the schedule because of a change in your staff's schedule. If you are trying to fill a part-time position using a flexible schedule it would be easier to hire a person who is unemployed or has another job that is flexible enough to accommodate your schedule. It is nice to have a part-time staff person who can be added into the schedule whenever needed.

Religion

Your staff will probably be members of many different religions. Be sure that you are sensitive to the needs of your staff and also serve the needs of your patrons. When you interview new staff, always tell the potential candidate what the days and hours of the job are. Make sure each candidate can fulfill the obligations of the position. If there are days when their religious beliefs prevent them from working, make sure that you can accommodate their needs. It is not fair to hire someone then hold it against them if they are unable to work certain days. If the position is part time, perhaps you can work around their days of observances. Some religions do not celebrate birthdays or holidays. Be sensitive to this when your branch celebrates such occasions. Don't make those people feel isolated by only having parties during the holidays. Have a luncheon or some other function to celebrate a job well done for the entire staff.

Friends Visiting

Do not allow staff to make a habit of inviting friends and family to visit them at work. It is distracting to everyone and work is not being done while friends are visiting. Talk to staff at a meeting about this if it gets to be a problem. Suggest that friends come at lunchtime and they all go out together. Do not allow staff to bring their young children to work with them. If the children are young enough to need a babysitter it is better for the parent to stay home with the children than to bring them to work. I had a situation once where a substitute came in to work on a Saturday and brought her four young children with her. They were all too young to be unsupervised and they ran around the library while she ignored them and worked at the circulation desk. Talk to your staff and let them know what is and is not acceptable. Totally unacceptable situations include the following:

1. Staff giving their spouse or partner a key to the building.
2. Staff having their friends go into the workroom without another staff member being present.
3. Staff bringing and leaving children with staff even if they are your staff's own children.
4. Staff letting friends or family use the workroom computers to check their e-mail.
5. Staff having friends eat lunch in the library's break room.

6. Staff inviting friends to library luncheons.

7. Staff having friends ask for special favors; for example, to be hired, to waive their fines, to delete lost items.

Accidents at Work

There will probably come a time when one of your staff members gets hurt on the job. A staff member reached up to shelve a book and another book fell on her face and chipped a tooth. Another staff member hurt his toe when a book cart filled with books rolled over it. Know what your library's policy is regarding employee accidents. Make sure the incident is documented with the employee's name, date, and what happened. Does the library have a medical facility it sends employees to when accidents happen? Make sure the employee receives instructions from the doctor about any work restrictions following an accident. Check with your human resources department to make sure you have the correct Worker's Compensation information.

Keeping Staff Healthy

Most library workrooms are small. When several people are confined to a small area, it doesn't take long for germs and disease to spread. It is inevitable that staff will get sick, but there are some things you and your staff can do to decrease the spread of germs.

1. Place signs on the restroom doors reminding staff to wash their hands.

2. Periodically spray community telephones with disinfectant.

3. Make available bottles of antibacterial hand lotion to use while on the service desks.

4. Maintain a smoke-free environment.

5. Encourage sick employees to stay home until they are no longer contagious.

6. Keep a bottle of pain reliever available to staff.

7. Check the ventilation system to make sure fresh air is circulating.

Recognition

One of the most powerful tools for fixing—or preventing—problems of motivation and morale is public praise.

Employee of the Month

Instead of choosing an employee *you* think has done a good job, set up a box in the workroom labeled "Employee of the Month." Have slips printed asking staff for the nominee's name and why they think that person should be the employee of the month. Allow your staff to nominate each other. At the end of the month, read the entries and select a winner based on the information submitted. By having your employees nominate each other, the pressure is taken off you to choose a winner. Whoever is selected does not need to know who nominated them. Have special certificates printed, frames purchased, and gift certificates to local restaurants offered as prizes if possible. Ask local merchants to donate prizes to your program. Make the presentation at a special staff luncheon. Display the certificate and picture of the employee in a prominent location at the service desk where that person usually works. Have a button made that says "Employee of the Month" for them to wear.

Library Page of the Month

In an effort to motivate your library pages and to reward those that are doing a good job, establish a Library Page of the Month program. Each month, select a library page who has done a good job the month before. Print certificates from a publishing program and write his name on it. Ask the Friends of the Library if they would purchase frames for the certificates and money to provide small gifts for the recipient. A gift certificate to a local bookstore is one idea. Gather the staff together and present the certificate and gift to your page. Display each certificate until the end of the month. If possible, ask that page to provide a photograph of himself to display with the certificate. Display them in a prominent place in your library. You are letting your pages know that their jobs are very important.

Patron Comments

If your staff receives letters or favorable written comments from patrons, post them in a prominent place so that all staff may view them. If it was a verbal comment, tell other staff members what was said. It makes that employee feel good about herself and makes others strive to also receive favorable comments. Place a copy of any printed comments in your employee personnel file.

Security Guards

If your branch has a security guard, ask if there are written policies regarding his or her duties. Make sure the security guard understands what the individual needs are at your branch. Ask to see a copy of the job description that they were given by their agency. Know what to do in the event that they are sick or hurt. Should the agency be called? What hospital should they be taken to? What happens if your security guard does not come in? These are all questions that you need to find the answers to before the situation arises. Talk to your security guard about the duties you would like him or her to perform. Some duties that should definitely be in their job description include the following:

1. Patrolling inside and outside of the building.

2. Keeping daily logs of branch activity.

3. Patrolling staff and patron parking lots.

4. Calling the police when the need arises.

5. Handling problem patrons who cannot be calmed down by staff.

6. Supervising the opening and closing of the building.

Patrols

Ask your security guard to patrol the outside of the building at least once every half hour. Having the presence of the security guard on the grounds and parking lots should deter vandals. Patrolling the inside of the building on a constant basis is a good way to maintain the safety and security of patrons and staff. Patrons are less likely to destroy or deface library property when they know the security guards are on constant patrol. Most of our problems occur at the branch when the security guard is not there. Your security guard should record activity after every patrol.

If an incident does arise, the guard should record it on an incident report. All incident reports must include the name of the person involved, contact information, the date, the time, and a detailed account of what happened. Depending upon the crime rate in your area, you may want your security guard to escort employees into the building in the morning, accompany library pages to the book returns, and make sure that employees get to their cars safely at closing.

Make sure that your guard checks everything that is supposed to be secure at closing. Check the meeting rooms, the restrooms, and book stacks for patrons after closing. If there are any unattended children, they need to be encouraged to call for rides to come and pick them up. Announcements need to be made of the approaching closing time and the building should be secured. If you have an alarm system, make sure that it is engaged as you exit the building.

11

Computers and Other Equipment

Computerized Data

Make sure your employees are knowledgeable about all of the databases available in your library system. Everyone should attend all workshops related to new databases and procedures within the library system. Patrons often use more than one branch and they expect to have the same data available at every location. Although all services may not be available at each location, your staff should use those databases on a regular basis so that they are able to teach patrons how to use them.

Policies

All employees at your branch need to know the policies regarding all computer databases. Policies on issues such as printing must be the same for all patrons. If your library sets a limit on the number of copies that can be printed by each patron, make sure all employees know what the limit is. Questions such as the amount of time spent training patrons on the use of databases should be answered in your policy manual. Make sure your policy is written down so that your staff can refer to it.

Internet Access

If your library has Internet terminals available to the public, you should already have Internet policies and procedures in place. If your branch will be getting them, there are decisions that need to be made. Who will be allowed to access the Internet: Patrons with library cards? The general public? Will children be allowed to use the Internet without parental permission? How long will patrons be able to be online at any one time? Will reservations be taken? A waiting list kept? How many pages are they allowed to print? How will patrons sign up? Will there be a user agreement to sign? Will your branch offer basic Internet instruction classes for patrons? All of these questions must be answered before the situations present themselves. What will the penalty be for patrons who abuse the Internet policy? How many times per day can a patron sign up to use the Internet when others are waiting? Is there a troubleshooter at your branch who can fix minor problems with the computers and printers? Make sure that patrons know about your Internet policy before they use the Internet at your branch.

Filtering Software in Libraries

On June 26, 1997, the United States Supreme Court issued a sweeping reaffirmation of core First Amendment principles and held that communications over the Internet deserve the highest level of constitutional protection.

The Court's most fundamental holding is that communications on the Internet deserve the same level of constitutional protection as books, magazines, newspapers, and speakers on a street-corner soapbox. The Court found that the Internet "constitutes a vast platform from which to address and hear from a worldwide audience of millions of readers, viewers, researchers, and buyers," and that "any person with a phone line can become a town crier with a voice that resonates farther than it could from any soapbox."

For libraries, the most critical holding of the Supreme Court is that libraries that make content available on the Internet can continue to do so with the same constitutional protections that apply to the books on libraries' shelves.

The Court's conclusion that "the vast democratic fora of the Internet" merit full constitutional protection will also serve to protect libraries that provide their patrons with access to the Internet. The Court recognized the importance of enabling individuals to receive speech from the entire world and to speak to the entire world. Libraries provide those opportunities to many who would not otherwise have them. The Supreme Court's decision will protect that access.

The use in libraries of software filters which block constitutionally protected speech is inconsistent with the United States Constitution and federal law and may lead to legal exposure for the library and its governing authorities. The American Library Association affirms that the use of filtering software by libraries to block access to constitutionally protected speech violates the Library Bill of Rights.

WHAT IS BLOCKING/FILTERING SOFTWARE?

Blocking/filtering software is a mechanism to:

- Restrict access to Internet content, based on an internal database of the product, or;
- Restrict access to Internet content though a database maintained external to the product itself, or;
- Restrict access to Internet content to certain ratings assigned to those sites by a third party, or;

- Restrict access to Internet content by scanning content, based on a keyword, phrase or text string, or;

- Restrict access to Internet content based on the source of the information.

PROBLEMS WITH BLOCKING/FILTERING SOFTWARE

Publicly supported libraries are governmental institutions subject to the First Amendment, which forbids them from restricting information based on viewpoint or content discrimination.

Libraries are places of inclusion rather than exclusion. Current blocking/filtering software not only prevents access to what some may consider "objectionable" material, but also blocks information protected by the First Amendment. The result is that legal and useful material will inevitably be blocked. Examples of sites that have been blocked by popular commercial blocking/filtering products include those on breast cancer, AIDS, women's rights, and animal rights.

- Filters can impose the producer's viewpoint on the community.

- Producers do not generally reveal what is being blocked, or provide methods for users to reach sites that were inadvertently blocked.

- Criteria used to block content are vaguely defined and subjectively applied.

- The vast majority of Internet sites are informative and useful. Blocking/filtering software often blocks access to materials it is not designed to block.

- Most blocking/filtering software is designed for the home market. Filters are intended to respond to the preferences of parents making decisions for their own children. Libraries are responsible for serving a broad and diverse community with different preferences and views. Blocking Internet sites is antithetical to library missions because it requires the library to limit information access.

- In a library setting, filtering today is a one-size-fits-all "solution," which cannot adapt to the varying ages and maturity levels of individual users.

- One role of librarians is to advise and assist users in selecting information resources. Parents and only parents have the right and responsibility to restrict their own children's access—and only their own children's access—to library resources, including the Internet. Librarians do not serve *in loco parentis*.

- Library use of blocking/filtering software creates an implied contract with parents that their children *will not be able* to access material on the Internet that they do not wish their children read or view. Libraries will be unable to fulfill this implied contract, due to the technological limitations of the software, thus exposing themselves to possible legal liability and litigation.

• Laws prohibiting the production or distribution of child pornography and obscenity apply to the Internet. These laws provide protection for libraries and their users.

Educate yourself, your staff, library board, governing bodies, community leaders, parents, elected officials, etc., about the Internet and how best to take advantage of the wealth of information available. For examples of what other libraries have done, contact the ALA Public Information Office at *pio@ala.org*.

Uphold the First Amendment by establishing and implementing written guidelines and policies on Internet use in your library in keeping with your library's overall policies on access to library materials.

Promote Internet use by facilitating user access to Web sites that satisfy user interest and needs.

Create and promote library Web pages designed both for general use and for use by children. These pages should point to sites that have been reviewed by library staff.

Consider using privacy screens or arranging terminals away from public view to protect a user's confidentiality.

Provide information and training for parents and minors that reminds users of time, place, and manner restrictions on Internet use.

Establish and implement user behavior policies.

[*Whole Library Handbook 3*, by George Eberhart. Reproduced with permission.]

Instructional Offering

Offer the community instructional services such as classes on the online public access computer, Internet instruction, how to use the library, opening an e-mail account, sending attachments through e-mail, and using word-processing programs. Advertise these programs well in advance and allow patrons time to register for them. Offer the classes at different times of the day to accommodate working schedules. The more information you can give patrons, the more independent they will be in their research. Plan your classes for times when your library is not at its busiest. You want people to have computers available to work on during the class and to be taught as a group. Conducting Internet classes before your branch opens to the general public is one way to accomplish this. Instructing patrons on the use of the opacs (online public access catalogs) could be done in the evenings if your branch is quieter then or if you close at an early hour. Select a staff member who is very knowledgeable about whatever is being taught. Staff should be able to instruct effectively and answer any questions related to the class.

Computer Downtime

If your library is automated you will have procedures in place in the event the computer system goes down. Find out what your policy is. You will probably check books out manually. This involves recording patrons' library card numbers and the barcode numbers of each item that they are borrowing. You may be able to perform manual checkout on your PC if your computer has that feature. Books returned should be put aside until the computers come back up. It is best not to accept overdue fines during the downtime to prevent mistakes on patron's records. You don't want to accept money from a patron and not be able to immediately update their library record.

Troubleshooting Equipment

Make sure that you know how to troubleshoot all machines that are installed in your branch. No one expects you to fix a broken machine, but everyone should be able to clear paper jams, add paper, change the toner, and do routine functions on your copier, microform machines, and CD-ROM workstations. Make sure that you can do basic functions on the word processor or word-processing software on the computers. Patrons will need help saving to disk, spell checking, changing fonts, etc. Make sure that you are able to perform these functions before experimenting on a patron's twenty-page document. Make sure that you can quickly change the tape on the cash register and retrieve any totals that you need. You will need to balance your income at closing and the cash register tells you how much money you should have minus whatever amount you began with.

Calling for Service

If the staff member in charge of calling for repair service is not available, someone else needs to place the call. Never wait until someone returns from a day off to call for repair. Have service repair numbers posted where all staff can see them. Patrons get very frustrated when machines are out of order. The longer your machines are out of order, the more your patrons will complain. Some of your equipment that can get out of order may include the copier, microfilm, microfiche, Internet, word processing, database computers, and children's games on CD-ROM.

12

Managing the Branch, Part 1: Paperwork and Procedures

Start Off Slowly

During your first few months on the job you may feel overwhelmed. This is normal. It takes many librarians over a year to feel comfortable and secure in their positions. Give yourself time to learn everything that you need to know. You will be very busy. You will be learning about your library system, your staff, how to complete reports that are required, and how to make decisions that are best for you and your branch. Meet with each staff member. Get their views and ideas about how the branch is being managed. Ask them about their positions. Are they happy? If not, why? What are their career plans?

Go slowly. Don't make changes just to be making them. Take your time. Maybe things are working fine the way they are. If you make drastic changes in the very beginning your staff will resent you and your changes. You may be doing away with something that was suggested by one of your employees. Sit back, get to know your staff, and make changes slowly and with the knowledge of your employees. Don't make changes to the workroom when you are alone; when your staff come in and see everything rearranged, they will feel insecure. Talk to your staff about the best way to handle specific projects. Ask them what they think needs to be changed at the branch. They may suggest ideas better than your own.

Educate Yourself

Attend workshops on supervising, customer service, problem patrons, and anything related to any aspect of your job. You will learn a lot from these workshops. Take notes and apply them to your daily routine. Attend workshops offered by your library system. Rearrange your service desk schedule to make it easier for you to go. Most workshops are very informative. Check with your state library. They usually offer many workshops on an ongoing basis. Request to attend those workshops. Any workshop that will help you perform your job better is a good workshop to attend. Make sure you attend those workshops on branch management.

Join committees that you are very interested in, would like to learn more about, and can contribute ideas to. Committees are great vehicles of change. If there is a committee that you would like to join because you have some ideas about the subject that you think will help, then don't hesitate to join. Never join a committee just to have a place to go to get away from your branch. Also, don't join more than two committees simultaneously because you don't want to be so busy that you can't devote the time needed to be a useful member. Most committees involve some outside commitment. Don't avoid being on committees because you think that they are a waste of time. If there is a committee formed to resolve a problem and you are able to help but choose not to, don't complain about the results of the work done by the committee or about the original problem.

Policies and Procedures

Make sure that you and your staff have access to and understand all policies and procedures. Your staff, no matter how long they have been in the library system, will ask for clarification of policies. Don't just know how to do things, however; do them. Don't ask your staff to do something that you would not do yourself. When they see you stamping date-due cards or shelving books, they are less likely to complain about doing things that are not in their own job descriptions.

Library Policy Handbook

All library policies should be written down and available to all staff. Try to separate various policies and procedures into different binders. Label each binder and place them on shelves in the workroom. If a staff member needs to refer to the circulation policy, for example, she can go directly to it. If all policies are in one large binder it will be difficult to locate what you need. Even if the sections are labeled, staff might not read it because it would be too overwhelming. Also, if the policies are separated, more than one person can read them at a time. If possible, have a separate copy of each policy for your own use.

Paperwork

You will have a great deal of paperwork. You will have reports that are due on a regular basis and others that were unexpected. Give yourself plenty of time to complete your reports. Make sure that you check your grammar, spelling, and organization. After you have completed a rough draft of your report, type it. A handwritten report is very unprofessional. Make sure that it is neat and free of smudges. Remember, anything that you send from your branch reflects on you. Make sure that you meet all deadlines. If you can't meet a deadline let your boss know in advance. If you will be taking vacation during the time that your report is due, submit it before you leave.

Forms File

I have several folders in my file that are marked for specific forms. In that file I include copies of all forms used at the branch. If someone uses the last copy of a form, you have a master copy that more can be made from. When you need specific forms required for branch management duties, they are readily available. As forms become obsolete, remove and replace them with new forms. You don't want to submit the old forms when you should be using new ones.

Filing System

If you have a file cabinet, develop a filing system that makes it easy for you to find whatever you need. Have specific folders for all categories. Don't have a folder marked Circulation. Have a separate folder for Circulation policy, one for Circulation procedures, and another for Circulation meeting minutes. If you have only one folder, you will have to look through everything in that folder just to find what you need. The more specific your folders, the better organized you will be. Having specific folders saves time and it is more efficient. If someone asks you for a memo that was sent previously, you will want to be able to put your hands on it right away rather than looking through a large stack of papers.

Keep a separate file for each staff member with his/her name on it. Keep copies of correspondence relating to him/her in that file. Copies of human resources documents, promotional confirmation letters, vacation requests, and letters of reprimand should all be kept together. Anytime you need to retrieve information about any one of your staff, you have it all together. If possible, store those files in a cabinet that can be locked. They should not be placed anywhere where staff have access to them. Staff should not be able to retrieve any information about their coworkers.

Backup Copies

Make copies of everything, all reports, projects, memos, etc. In the event that something is lost or misdirected in the interdepartmental mail, you can send or fax another copy immediately. Also, the next time you have to do a similar report you will know what was sent previously. For example, if you sent your goals for the current year you can check your files, look at what you submitted last year and see how many goals you met. If some of those goals were not met, they can be incorporated into your new goals and objectives for the current year.

Weekly Schedule

The branch's weekly schedule should reflect the hours to be worked by each employee. It includes planned vacations, doctor appointments, and workshops. Some schedules also include the hours each employee is scheduled on the service desk. Every employee should receive a copy of the schedule so that they know when they are expected to be on the service desk. Post a copy of the schedule in a prominent place for everyone to refer to in the event of last-minute changes after the schedule has been distributed. When someone calls in sick, the schedule needs to reflect that change. The desk schedule also needs to be adjusted so that the person who is out sick has a replacement for their service desk hours. Your boss may ask for a copy of your schedule and any changes that occurred during the week.

Staff Directory

Ask for a Library-system staff directory which includes the names of all employees, their locations, positions, and telephone numbers. A directory listed by location is much easier because if you want to speak to someone in Human Resources at the main library, that person will be listed with all other administration employees. This is especially helpful if you are new to the library system and don't know everyone's name yet. You could speak directly to the person handling your particular situation without being transferred to different departments. Keep the directory listing on or near your desk so that it is always handy. I have a bulletin board above my telephone where I keep important telephone numbers. Make a copy and keep one with you at home; you may have to call a staff member in the evening.

Ask your staff to provide you with the names and telephone numbers of people to call in the event they have a medical emergency. If someone suddenly becomes ill, you will have a contact name and telephone number at your fingertips. Don't forget to include your own. Put the list in a place that is not displayed but where everyone can find it immediately.

Mailboxes for Staff

Order clear magazine-type files for each of your employees to use as an in-house mailbox. Have them shelved alphabetically by last name and kept in a convenient location in your workroom. Place memos, correspondence, and professional literature in the mailboxes for staff to receive. Do not place confidential information in employee mailboxes.

Staff Calendar

Order a large desk calendar on which your staff is to record upcoming doctor appointments, vacations, staff parties, and workshops. When everything is recorded on one calendar, it is immediately apparent which days you will be short staffed. If someone wants to request vacation time, they can see who else is planning vacation for the same time period.

Answering Machine

If your library uses an answering machine, it should always play recorded messages for patrons to hear when your library is closed. There should be a separate telephone line for staff to use to call in sick or let someone know they will be late. Ask a staff member who has a pleasant voice to record the outgoing message. Tell patrons which library they are calling, the location, hours, and any closings that are coming up soon. Ask them to call back when you are open. If your library does not have an answering machine, ask the administration if one can be purchased for your branch.

Payroll

Payroll is one area where you will not want to make any mistakes. Not doing the payroll correctly could result in your staff either not being paid at all or being paid incorrectly. Make sure your payroll forms contain all the required information and signatures. Make sure that they are submitted by the deadline set by the human resources department. Recheck to be sure that you have the correct number of hours on the correct days. Always make a copy of the payroll forms. If for some reason they are not received by the department requesting them, you can deliver or fax another copy without going back and researching everyone's work schedule again.

Circulation Statistics: More Is Better

Circulation statistics are the number of items checked out from your branch within a certain period of time. Usually, the larger your branch the greater your circulation statistics will be. Compare your branch to others of similar size in your library system. Your branch may circulate more or fewer items per month depending on many factors. Some of these factors may include the following:

1. Proximity of your branch to schools, businesses, and residential areas.
2. Hours of operation.
3. Number of programs and services.
4. Level of customer service.
5. Literacy level of the community.

If your circulation statistics are low, you can increase them by changing some of the above factors. You can't change the location of your branch, but you can advertise to increase awareness of your location. If your branch closes before patrons leave work in the afternoon, ask the administration to consider extending the operating hours of your branch. Take a look at your programs and services. Do you offer storytime for preschoolers? After-school homework help? Free income-tax service? Patrons may come to the library for the first time to attend a program and decide to become regular users. Are your employees providing friendly service? Word of mouth about your branch can increase the number of users, which in turn increases your circulation. Offer literacy classes at your branch. There may be many segments of the community that you are not reaching.

Think of other ways to increase your circulation statistics. Anything that you can do to invite more people into your branch will increase your statistics. Plan programs that you have not offered before. Ask managers of busy branches what they are doing to increase circulation statistics. Invite school groups to come and have a tour or storytime. Register the children for library cards ahead of time so they can borrow books when they come. Have displays of books set up around the library to encourage patrons to borrow more books and materials. Visit bookstores and look around to see how their books are displayed. Display as many books with the covers facing patrons as possible. Display new books before they are shelved with the rest of the collection. Publish the titles of new books and other media in a newsletter that you publish each month. Find out what current movies are showing in the local theatres. If any are based on books, feature those books. Is your branch hard to find? Contact your local newspaper and ask if they would feature your library in an article. Offer services for free that other organizations charge a fee for. For example, during tax season, offer free income-tax help by trained volunteers such as the AARP.

Recording Statistics

Make sure that you and your staff record statistics of all work done at the branch. This is especially true of public service duties. Most library systems must keep statistics of items borrowed, reserves taken, reserves filled, etc. See what the policy is for your library system. Your statistics are very important because they are an indicator of how well your branch is used: how many patrons visit, what genres they borrow most, etc. Statistics can be used to justify a larger materials budget, an increase in staff, or even a larger facility. Make sure that your statistics are as accurate as possible and encourage your staff to make a habit of recording them.

Budget

If you are responsible for ordering your own materials, at the beginning of each fiscal year divide the amount that is allotted for each category by the total number of times you will submit orders to the acquisitions or collection development department. Use these figures as guides to budget your funds for the entire year. Don't just blindly order without keeping track of how much you are spending or without staying within a budget. It is very easy to spend your entire budget in just a few months if you are not careful.

You probably have several budgets for your branch. You may or may not know the exact amount of money budgeted for your branch but you should try to spend conservatively. This includes ordering supplies, books, materials, periodicals, and printing needs. Don't order what you don't need or cannot justify. Use the guidelines set forth by the administration when placing any orders.

Annual Reports

If your library requires you to submit annual reports each year, go through your monthly reports to get information to submit. Your annual report should not be a large document covering everything that happened at your branch. It should highlight exceptional programs or initiatives at your branch. For example, if your circulation statistics have risen by 10 percent, say so; don't just say what your circulation statistics were. Include programs with higher-than-average attendance, new programs, new staff, anything that you did that perhaps no other branch did. Don't include anything negative.

Capital Requests

Capital requests are requests for items that are over a monetary limit set by your library administration. For example, a capital request might be for items costing over $1000. If your branch needs new carpeting, an extension to the parking lot, or new furniture, those would all be considered capital items. The best thing to do is to keep a file marked "capital requests" and write down what you need to improve your branch. That way, when it comes time to submit those requests, you won't forget anything. Make sure you research your requests with current prices and detailed justifications. If your library is small, your boss may submit requests on your behalf. Let him/her know what your branch needs. When deciding what items you would like for your branch, always consider your patrons. Anything that would improve service to the public or make patrons more comfortable can be justified on that basis.

Minor Requests

Minor requests are those that are below the monetary amount set by your library system. If $1000 or more is the capital request amount, then minor requests are those items that will cost less than $1000. Those items may include book carts, book display racks, or a microwave oven for your break room. Request only what you feel is needed at your branch and make sure that those requests, too, are justified. Don't be discouraged if you don't get what you need the first time you submit a request. You are not the only manager making requests. The library system looks at all requests submitted and places priorities on those requests. It may take a few years to get everything.

Structural Requests

Structural requests are improvements needed to the physical structure of your building. Painting, wallpaper, pressure washing, and door replacements are all examples of structural requests. Record any problems that need attention. Look at your lighting. Is the branch well lit? Do you need new lighting? Do the heating/air conditioning ducts need to be cleaned? Does the circulation desk need to be refinished? Listen to patron comments and complaints about the branch. Make sure that your branch looks the best it can. Make your requests and see what happens. Anything that is structurally a part of your branch should be evaluated annually for improvement. Your branch should always look neat, clean, and inviting. Don't wait until the walls are a mess before you request that they be painted. It may take a few years for your request to be approved; in the meantime, you will have a very unattractive library. As soon as you notice something that needs to be done, make a note so that you can request it when the time comes.

Don't make excuses like "I won't get anything for this branch; there is no sense in asking." It is your responsibility to make the requests. The administration will decide what you get and when.

Substitute Staffing

Substitutes are employees who are hired to fill in at various libraries on an as-needed basis. If you have a vacancy or someone who is out on extended sick leave, that is a good justification for using a substitute. If your library system uses substitutes you should follow these guidelines:

1. Read your library's policy on using substitutes.

2. Request permission to use a substitute from the appropriate staff member in the administration. It may be the human resources/personnel department or it may be your boss.

3. After getting approval, call the substitute to see if he is available on the day that you need him.

4. When the substitute arrives, make sure that he signs in, noting the time he arrived, and sign out when he leaves.

5. Make sure every substitute gets the correct number of hours worked submitted to the payroll department. You want to make sure that they are all paid correctly.

6. Make sure that you use a substitute only if you absolutely need one. If you have a vacancy but have other employees who can change their schedules around to make sure the desk is covered, allow them to do so. It takes a lot of money to keep the substitute pool operating well enough to be able to aid all of the branches that need assistance. Don't use any more funds than you need to. If you request substitutes when you really don't need them then one day you will really need a substitute and you may not get approval. Let the administration be assured that if you request a substitute you must really need one because you are not one to abuse the library system.

Cross Train Your Staff

Training your staff to work in different departments, or cross training, is to everyone's advantage. Staff members learn to do jobs that may give them additional experience when applying for promotions. When the branch is short staffed, you can pull people from other departments to help out. Obviously not everyone can work in every department, but all staff can and should be trained to work at the circulation desk. Reference staff should be trained to work in their own department, in Circulation, and in the Children's Department. They probably will not do storytimes as this task takes more training and experience. Moreover, only reference librarians should work the reference desk because knowing how and where to find information is an essential part of working at this desk. If someone calls in sick and you can't find a substitute, being able to pull staff from one department to work in another is a great alternative. You as a manager must be able to work at all three service desks. You get to know the jobs, your patrons, and you can suggest changes to be made to procedures at the desk.

13

Managing the Branch, Part 2: The Infrastructure

Power Outages

There will be times when the weather or some other source will cause you to have a power outage at your branch. Have procedures in place in the event it happens. Have flashlights available at each service desk and in the workroom and to help patrons locate books. Patrons don't usually leave the branch when the power goes out. Most of the time if the power goes out in the community, more patrons come to your branch, either because they think your power is on or because they don't have anything else to do. Always encourage patrons doing word processing to save their documents regularly. I have seen patrons typing a twenty-page document without saving it when the library either has a power surge or the power is out for several minutes. They try desperately to retrieve their document to no avail. At the circulation desk, in addition to manual checkout, offer patrons assistance in finding materials in the book stacks. All reference staff should have a basic knowledge of the Dewey decimal system so they won't be totally dependent upon electronic sources. Practice helping patrons to gather information when the power is on so your staff will be trained if the power goes out.

Book Donations

Patrons love to donate books to the library. Find out what your library's policy is on accepting donated books. Obviously not every donated book can or should be added to the collection. The condition of donated books received ranges from brand-new books that are on your reserve list to moldy, insect-infested books that have spent years in someone's attic. When books are received, explain to patrons that not all donated books will be added to the collection. Once a book is donated, it becomes the property of the library to be used deemed appropriate. Some may be sold in a book sale, some added to the collection, and others may be discarded. The Friends of the Library may accept books in good condition to sell at their book sale.

Books that are mildewed need to be discarded immediately. Mildew is very contagious and it will spread throughout your collection and damage your books if you are not careful.

If you have forms for patrons to sign acknowledging that they donated books for tax purposes, it is not a good idea to allow staff to place a monetary value on the form for the books. If the patron is audited, you don't want to be placed in a position where you are verifying the value of their charitable gift.

Stamping Date-Due Cards

If your branch stamps date-due cards, make absolutely sure that the correct date is being stamped on the cards. It is a good idea to figure out the due dates ahead of time and place them on the large desk-sized calendar. That way, anyone stamping will stamp the same date. Take into account days that the library is closed. Stamp the date clearly without smudging. Use a large stamp so that the due date is clearly visible. If you are stamping for the next year, make sure you turn the year on the stamp as well as the month and date. Have cards stamped at least a week ahead of time. On slow days, have staff stamp date-due cards as a part of their off-desk duties. Never wait to stamp cards until the day before they are to be used. Your branch may be busy and no one will have time to stamp cards.

Checking in the Mail

If your library is automated and you can process your mail through the computer, you should definitely take advantage of it. When patrons ask whether or not an issue of a magazine came in, instead of going to the shelves and looking everywhere for it, you can just check the computer and see whether it arrived and when it was checked in. It also makes it easier to claim missing issues that did not arrive. You could also add notes to the record in the database so that anyone checking in the mail would know what to do with that particular periodical. For example, if the classifieds are removed from the Sunday newspaper to be kept at the information desk, that information could be included in the notes. You will also know right away if you received a duplicate issue.

Periodicals

The periodicals in your branch are a special part of your collection that must be constantly maintained to be a useful part of your library. Some periodicals are for research, some for pleasure. When purchasing new periodicals try to focus on the needs of your patrons. See where the gaps are in your collection. If your branch is located near a beach, make sure you have magazines pertaining to surfing and boating. If your branch is located near the mountains, order camping and hiking periodicals. Don't order periodicals only because you like them personally; your patrons may not be interested in them. If you are originally from a small town in another state, don't order that town's local newspaper just because you want to read it. Order a personal subscription and read it at home. Your branch should have a core collection of periodicals plus others that will be used by your community.

Keep a file for periodical requests made by patrons. When a patron asks you to order a certain subscription for your branch, place any information about it in the file. You can get information about the publications from *Magazines for Libraries,* by Bill and Linda Sternberg *Katz.*

If you have periodicals in your collection that are rarely used, cancel those subscriptions and purchase something that will receive more usage. You will know the ones used the most because they will be lying all over the tables and chairs in the reading area. If you are unsure about whether a subscription is used or not, pull it from the shelves temporarily and see if anyone asks about it. If that is not practical or if you have many subscriptions that you are unsure about, attach a note to the shelves asking patrons to indicate by tally mark on the note if they read that publication. At the end of a period of time that you determine, count the tally marks. One patron in a two-month period is not enough to justify the cost of the subscription and the maintenance of the back issues.

When requesting new periodicals, make sure you have all of the information needed to submit them for approval: price, frequency, holdings in the system, publisher, and justification for your branch.

Claimed Periodicals

When your staff checks in periodicals, make a note as to any issues not received. Contact the person in the library system in charge of purchasing and renewing the subscriptions. Let them know the title and issues that are missing. They will put in a claim to receive either the missing issues or a credit to your subscription.

Maintenance

Your branch library must be maintained. Burned-out light bulbs, continuously running toilets, out-of-order copier machines are just a few of the items that must be addressed. The rule of thumb is to report any maintenance problem as soon as it is discovered. If you have access to e-mail, send a message to the person in charge of processing work orders for the maintenance department. These include your building, grounds, and parking lots. Display telephone numbers for repair services for machines in the workroom so that all staff know where to find them. When the copier breaks down during income-tax season for example, you need to quickly call for service. If you have an emergency that needs immediate attention, call the maintenance contact person to report the problem. If they are unavailable, make sure you talk to someone else in that department so that it can be taken care of immediately. If the heating or air conditioning unit is out of order or if patrons can't use the restroom, that is an emergency.

Missing Parts to AV Materials

Frequently when patrons check out audiovisual materials, they forget to return parts of the item. For example, if a book on tape contains five cassettes, they might return four and leave the remaining tape in their machine. As soon as it is discovered that part of the set is missing, don't check it in! Search the computer to see who returned it and give them a call. When calling the patron make sure it's on the same day you receive the item. Either talk to the patron or leave a message to let them know they forgot to return part of the item. Be very pleasant and professional. Never accuse a patron of not returning an item on purpose. If the item with a missing part was left on the counter, the patron is probably still in the building. Add a note to their library record to ask them about the missing tape. If the item was checked in and you don't know who had it, put it aside with a note indicating that part of the set is missing. Don't re-shelve it until the missing part is returned. Enter a note in the computer so that patrons checking for availability will know that that copy is not available for checkout. Once the missing item is returned and placed in its original case, remove all notes from the item and the patron's record.

Pay Telephone

If you constantly have patrons asking to use your telephone, you should talk to the administration about having a pay telephone installed at your branch. The telephone should be placed either in your lobby or just outside of the library building. We have had numerous patrons asking to use the telephone to return calls from beepers, to arrange meetings, and to call for rides home. We refer all patrons to our pay telephones unless they are children calling home for a ride. If you have only one telephone line, you especially need a pay telephone. Every patron who is talking on your branch's telephone is preventing you from serving other patrons who try to call in. If you have a situation where a patron needs to use your telephone and you don't have a pay telephone, tell them to limit the call to five minutes or less. If the patron is not off of the telephone within five minutes, let him know that he has to end the telephone call. If he refuses, pick up the extension, identify yourself, and tell both parties that you are sorry but they must end the call.

Cellular Telephones

Many libraries have problems with patrons either allowing their cellular telephones to ring continuously or patrons who talk on their cellular telephones in the building. I have seen patrons call family members to tell them the titles of DVDs that we have available. Cellular telephones disturb patrons who are reading, studying, or just browsing the shelves. Place signs on the front door and inside the building telling patrons to take cellular telephone calls outside the building or in the lobby. If they don't read the signs or if they use their cellular telephones anyway, walk over to them and politely let them know that they should go outside. Most patrons will comply.

Income-Tax Season

From January 1 through April 15, libraries that participate in distributing tax forms or offering free tax assistance are especially busy. Helping patrons to locate forms that they need without offering tax advice is very difficult. From patrons who take one of each form whether they need them or not, to patrons looking for forms for their specific occupations, tax season is stressful for everyone. I'm sure that you will have patrons who come into the library the evening of April 15 searching for specific forms that are only available directly from the IRS. When ordering tax forms in the fall to be distributed during tax season, always order more than you think you will need. Post signs telling when tax assistance will be available and what forms have not yet arrived.

Patron Accidents

There may come a time when there will be an emergency at your branch involving a patron. A patron may feel sick, fall on the library's property, or need you to call the police for one reason or another. It is a very stressful moment for both patron and staff so you need to know ahead of time what to do so that all policies and procedures are followed. If a patron feels sick, ask them what is the matter. Offer them a chair to sit in if they want to. Offer to call family members for them. Many patrons will want the least amount of attention drawn to them as possible. If after a few minutes they are not feeling any better or if they feel worse, call the emergency medical service (EMS) at 911 immediately. If they are examined and medical personnel determine that they are okay and can be taken home by a family member, allow them to do so. Get as much information from the patron as possible. Get their name, telephone number, closest relative's name and telephone number, and the nature of the illness. If they cannot or will not give a lot of information, ask for their library card and get the information that you need that way. Use their personal information only to notify family members of their situation. If they are transported to the hospital, make sure that you are able to contact a family member to let them know what happened. Call back a few days later to see how they are doing.

If a patron falls on library property, follow the same procedures except if they complain of any type of injury. In that case you should call medical personnel immediately whether they want you to or not. If the patron later decides to sue the library it will be documented that you did everything that you could to care for them. Make sure that you write a detailed incident report every time there is a situation at your branch where the police or ambulance is called. This is especially crucial when a patron is involved.

Incident Reports

Incident reports are written documentation that describe a particular event. Your library system may have a specific form for you to use to document any incident that occurs at your branch that needs to be reported. If there is an accident or emergency involving one of your staff, know what the procedures are ahead of time. There will be no time to look for memos or to call other staff to tell you what to do. Know which medical facility handles workers' compensation claims and accidents on the job. After your staff has been taken care of, complete the incident report immediately. You will remember all of the details and any witnesses involved will probably still be available. Make sure you include the name of the staff member, the date, day, and time of the incident. Describe in exact detail what happened and what was done to help. When incidents happen to patrons, get as much information from them as possible—name, address, telephone number, person to call about their emergency—along with the information gathered in the staff emergency incident report. Call your boss and tell him what happened. E-mail or send the incident report to the human resources department. If a patron falls or complains about being sick with pain, dizziness, or a chronic medical condition, call an ambulance immediately! Time may be crucial especially since you don't know how long the person felt sick before they told you. Most librarians are not doctors; we are not to interview patrons to discover the nature of the ailment nor to hope that the patron feels better. Even if the patron does not want an ambulance called, it is in your best interest to do everything possible to help them. You will be glad you went the extra mile if your library system is sued by an injured patron.

Parking Lot

If you have a security guard, ask her to check your parking lot often for potholes, overhanging trees, or broken glass. Ask her to go out at night and make sure all lights are on. Ask your security guard to patrol the parking lot periodically. Report anything that patrons complain about or that you notice that needs to be taken care of.

Polling Place

If you have a separate meeting room and you are looking for ways to increase your circulation, you might consider making your branch a polling place on election day. Talk to the local or county voter registration department for information on how to become a polling place. Have an instructional program before election day to teach people how to use the voting booth. Have a booth delivered in advance so that patrons who are voting for the first time know what to expect. Ask an experienced poll manager to conduct the program and be able to answer questions. Prospective voters coming to your program may become new patrons. Any opportunity to acquire new users should be explored. Talk to other facilities that are polling places. Ask them what if any problems have arisen in the past. If you do decide to become a polling place, make sure someone is available to be there early to open the building and someone else to close the building if voting goes past operating hours.

Acrylic Displays

Displays are used in libraries to increase circulation or to communicate a message to patrons. Clear acrylic displays work well for books and media. Patrons can see at a glance what is available and everything is housed in a neat unit. Fast-moving items such as DVDs, videocassettes, books on compact disk, books on audiotape, and music compact disks tend to be easier to maintain in displays than on the shelves. Indeed, shelving them has many disadvantages. Media tend to fall from the shelves easily because of their small size; they get trapped between shelves and are easily missed when one is looking for them; media get out of order quickly because patrons tend to browse, pick them up, and put them back in any open space. Also, that area of the collection will tend to be crowded with patrons standing in the same spot rather than being able to move around to different display units. Stationary units are better, even though you need more room for people to walk around them, because you don't want one person spinning the display when another is viewing the other side.

Display Cases

If you have a glass display case, use it to showcase items of interest to the community. Call community groups and individuals who collect specific items. Ask if they would like to display items in your case to be viewed by your patrons. Only borrow and display items that can be secured and kept locked in your case.

Have the owner sign a form not holding the library responsible for stolen or damaged items. When the owner comes to bring their items, it is better to have him or her place the items in the display case. Don't allow staff to help; something might get broken. When the owner is finished filling the case with the items, lock the case. Display books pertaining to those items next to the case. Have a sign placed in the display case with the name and telephone number of the person to contact for more information about the displayed items.

Notary Public

Some libraries offer free notary service. Ask the administration if they would pay for your training and equipment. Place a sign where it is visible to the public indicating that you offer free notary service. People who come in to have something notarized may decide to become new users. Have your notary ask the patron getting a document notarized if they have a library card. Tell them to tell their friends to come and use the library. Let them know about all of the services and materials available to them.

Temporary Closing

If your branch library needs to be closed temporarily for any length of time, there are many things you need to do in preparation for the closing. If your branch will be renovated and you are not able to work in the building, you must make definite plans for your staff and branch materials. For example, if your branch will be closed for two months for renovation, here are just a few of the decisions that will have to be made:

1. How many staff will work on discharging books placed in your book return?
2. Which branch will your staff be working from?
3. Will any of your staff help at other branches?
4. What will your library pages be doing during the renovation?
5. Who will telephone all of the parents of storytime children of possible cancellation of storytimes?
6. Who will call the janitorial staff?
7. What happens to patron reserves that should be picked up at your branch?
8. Who will pick up the mail from the post office?
9. Where will the returned items be stored?
10. Who will notify the media of the branch's closing?
11. Who will contact patrons in book clubs, groups that booked the meeting rooms, volunteers, and regularly scheduled groups that visit the branch?

12. Will you allow staff to take vacation time during the closing period?

13. Who will process new books for your branch?

There are many other issues that must be considered when your branch closes. Sometimes when staff find out that the branch is closing, they are excited because they see it as an automatic vacation. You actually work harder when your branch is closed, however. Once the branch closes, in addition to taking care of the items listed above, you have to keep checking on the progress of your branch. Do not allow staff to take the entire closing time for vacation. They should each stagger a week or two off if you have a large staff. You will need help in making sure that all items are processed during the closing.

If your branch is closing suddenly because of weather, you won't have time to notify patrons. If you have an answering machine, change the message to reflect your closing because of weather and ask patrons to listen to the media for reopening dates. Place a sign on your book return and front doors notifying patrons that they will not be charged overdue fees for books due during your closing period.

Inclement Weather

On days of inclement weather, you need to decide how and when to empty the book return. You can't always wait until the rain or snow stops falling. The weather may be bad all day. If your book return has a bin that is removable, it should be brought into the library to be emptied. Have large sheets of clear plastic ready to place over the entire cart so the materials don't get wet. Be sure to leave the book return's door open while the bin is removed so that patrons do not place materials in there. If your book return does not have a removable bin, either the materials will have to be removed while the cart is covered in plastic or you will have to wait until the next day and backdate the books that were not removed. If there is a threat of extremely bad weather and the library will be closed, lock the book return and place a sign on it. On the sign, tell patrons to hold on to their materials and they will not be charged a late fee. If you don't lock the book return, patrons will continue to add books to it even if the books are hanging out of the book return.

Book-Return Procedure

Your library pages need to be trained in the correct way to empty your book return. If all library pages empty it the same way, it will be much easier for your circulation staff to discharge and sort the returned items. The library pages should empty the book return as quickly as possible while continuing to be as efficient as possible. The following is the procedure I trained my library pages to use:

1. All books are placed on the cart right side up, spines facing outward. No books upside down.

2. All books and materials in like categories are grouped together. For example, all paperbacks together, all adult nonfiction together, all children's picture books together, etc.

3. When patrons drive up with more items, library pages should accept them, thank the patrons, and place the items on the book cart where they belong.

When the book cart is rolled in, the books and materials are already sorted. After they are discharged they can either be shelved, placed on book carts to be shelved, or placed on sorting shelves.

The number of times a day that you empty your book return depends upon how busy your facility is and how long it takes the book return to fill up. If you are at a small branch with not much activity, once a day is probably enough. If you are at a busy branch you should empty it more often. Our branch circulates about 40,000 items per month so we empty the book returns three times daily. Make sure the book return is emptied at least daily. If that is not possible, make sure that you backdate your computer to reflect the last date that the book return was emptied.

Janitorial Staff

Your janitorial staff is an important part of your branch. It is their job to make sure the building is clean, all of the trash emptied, and restrooms replenished with supplies. An incompetent staff will have patrons complaining about dirty tables, trash on the grounds, and dirty bathrooms. I have had situations at my branch where angry patrons came out of the restroom to report that there was no toilet paper. Not only was there no toilet paper in the restrooms, there were no extra rolls at the branch! You do not want to have to explain to a patron why there wasn't any available. People do steal toilet paper that is left lying around, but if the janitorial staff puts paper products in their holders and checks supplies each night, that incident should not happen. Talk to the supervisor of your janitorial staff. Keep in contact with him/her and report any problems immediately. Don't wait until a problem has gone on for weeks before reporting it. Also, get a copy of the list of janitorial duties and the frequency at which they are to be done. If the staff should dust and vacuum every night and you notice that it isn't being done, report this to the supervisor. In addition to reporting it, document the date and the problem being reported.

If you or your staff notice that things are being done that should not be, such as touching items on staff's desks, eating food from the staff refrigerator, etc., these, too, should be reported. If possible, drop in on the janitorial staff unannounced and see if they are doing what they should. I know of a case where a janitor brought his dog to the library every night and the carpet became infested with fleas. Another company hired a woman who did not have a babysitter. She was trying to clean the building with a crying baby less than a year old lying on the break-room couch. Get to know the janitorial staff. Let them know that you expect them to fulfill their obligations to your branch.

There should be an area in your branch where the janitorial staff can store their equipment and supplies. Not only is it easier for them to have their equipment readily accessible, you may need to borrow some supplies to clean up an unexpected mess. You need to have your janitorial staff's daytime telephone numbers to let them know about anything they need to make sure they take care of. Remember that the janitorial staff has a key to your branch. They need to be responsible for closing up the branch when they are finished and resetting the alarm if needed.

Courier Services

Unless you are the manager of a stand-alone library, you will have courier service that delivers books and interdepartmental mail on a regular basis.

The couriers are your direct delivery to everyone in the library system. They pick up and deliver books, materials, and interdepartmental mail for the library system. The couriers have a difficult and strenuous job that they must perform everyday in all types of weather. Don't look down upon them as if they were incompetent people with low intelligence. They deserve to be respected in their positions, as do all employees in the library system.

Make sure that when the courier arrives you have everything ready. All book crates should be labeled clearly with their destination branch name. Make sure that the crates are not overfilled and that they are stackable. Don't make the courier wait while you finish typing a report that is due that day. He has many stops to make and you will be delaying the schedule. If he is supposed to take the bank deposit that day, have a sign posted in the workroom so no one forgets to give it to him. It is the staff's responsibility to make sure that he/she gets it. The bank deposit should not be left out until the courier arrives. It is not the courier's responsibility to ask you for the bank deposit. He is not expected to know which day the deposit is due for every branch.

Supplies

Make sure that you have adequate supplies before you place an order. Essentials like cash register tape, copier paper, library cards, etc., should never run out. On the other hand, don't stockpile more supplies than you will ever use. If you do, your allotted supply budget will be depleted before the end of the fiscal year. You may need to order something new or the library may cease to use something that you have stockpiled. Track the number of boxes or packages of each item your branch uses per month to estimate the number that should be ordered per ordering period.

Supplies Inventory

Appoint one of your staff to be in charge of ordering, inventory, and distribution of supplies. Ask him or her to inventory all the supplies currently at your branch. If possible, keep all supplies in one place. Make a chart listing all supplies ordered, number available, number needed, date ordered, date received, number received, and whether or not an item was backordered. Keep the original chart in a safe place and copy or print more copies from the computer. The chart will prevent you from suddenly discovering that you have run out of something you use every day. Keeping track of your supplies also deters staff from taking more than they need of any one item.

Keep supplies in a central location in view of all staff. It makes the supplies available to everyone and easier for staff to communicate immediately when they have taken the next-to-last of anything.

What to Do If You Are Served with a Subpoena

You are a librarian approached by a police officer and served with a subpoena, compelling you to produce patron records identifying the names of all patrons who have borrowed books on childbearing in the last nine months. Farfetched? Impossible? Unfortunately, it is neither of those things. It happened several years ago. Fortunately, the librarian, with the assistance of the city attorney and the support and cooperation of her library board, was able to convince a court that the subpoena should be "quashed," a legal term meaning that she did not need to comply with the subpoena request.

What should you do if you are served with a subpoena requesting information about patron records or if you are simply asked to supply such information without a subpoena request? Whether the request comes from a law enforcement authority or a private individual or group involved in litigation, you should take the same steps. As an initial matter, inform the requester that you cannot comply without consulting with an attorney. A subpoena generally does not require an immediate response, but rather provides a response date some time in the future.

Although the response time may only be days away and a requester may otherwise demand immediate compliance, you should never provide patron borrowing information without consulting an attorney. There are important reasons why you must exercise caution.

First, many states have specific statutes that protect patron borrowing information and designate such information as confidential. In those states, it is a statutory violation to produce identifiable patron information to persons other than library employees engaged in their regular library duties, unless there is a court order compelling the library to produce such information. A subpoena is not a court order. Although it will have a court caption and appear to be an official court document, it is, in fact, issued at the request of an attorney or law-enforcement officer and is not reviewed by a judge prior to issuance.

Increasingly, libraries are also maintaining video collections for patron use. It is a violation of federal law to produce information related to borrowing of videos. The Video Privacy Protection Act prohibits the disclosure of information about video use. This federal law applies in every state.

Second, producing patron borrowing information is harmful to First Amendment concerns, whether or not a state particularly designates such information as confidential. Release of patron borrowing information impacts First Amendment concerns. If patrons believed that their reading material would be subject to public scrutiny, the exercise of their First Amendment rights would be chilled. Patrons would refrain from reading material on controversial issues or sensitive topics if they believed that their choice of reading material would become the subject of public exposure and scrutiny. Your library should develop a confidentiality policy concerning patron borrowing information and publicize that policy to your patrons.

Third, the request may be overly broad and burdensome to the resources of the library. Irrespective of First Amendment concerns and statutory provisions, a subpoena may be quashed if it is unduly burdensome. Law enforcement officials may be conducting legitimate investigations, but the breadth and scope of their requests may trample important First Amendment rights without a compelling need for the requested information. Only a court can conduct the necessary balancing test to determine if there is a sufficiently compelling need for the information to justify the production of confidential patron borrowing information. The library should be involved in those court proceedings to fully apprise the court of the important First Amendment rights at stake if disclosure is permitted.

For example, in the case requesting patron information regarding books on childbearing, law-enforcement officials were conducting a legitimate inquiry into a child abandonment case. There was, however, no reason to believe that the person who had abandoned a newborn baby had borrowed books from the library on childbearing prior to committing the criminal act. There was every reason to believe that people who had committed no crimes and borrowed books on childbearing would be subject to interrogation based simply on their choice of reading material. The law enforcement officials were engaged in a fishing expedition. Recognizing the important First Amendment rights at stake and the failure of the law enforcement officials to demonstrate a compelling need for the information, the court in that case concluded that the librarian was not required to comply with the subpoena.

In some cases, law enforcement officials may have a legitimate need for patron borrowing information. In those cases, the court will issue a "court order" requiring the library to produce such information. A library should consult an attorney even if it receives a court order to determine the propriety of an appeal. If the library has not been involved in the proceedings before the court, it is likely that the judge would not have had a complete presentation of the important First Amendment issues. However, the library and librarian would not be violating any statutory protection of patron borrowing information by releasing information pursuant to a court order.

In the absence of a court order requiring a librarian to produce such confidential information, the librarian must maintain the confidentiality of patron borrowing information to protect the First Amendment rights at stake in such a situation and to comply with any applicable state or federal protections of such information. If you are confronted with a request for patron borrowing information, always seek legal advice.

[*Whole Library Handbook 3,* by George Eberhart. Reproduced with permission.]

Bomb Threat

Most library systems have specific procedures for what to do in the event that someone calls in a bomb threat. You will want to signal another staff member to dial 911 while you keep the caller on the telephone. Write down everything he says and get as much information from him as possible. When the police arrive, they will give you further instructions. Everyone should leave quickly without panic and not come back into the building until the authorities say that it is okay to return.

Preservation of Materials

Drying Water-Damaged Collections

SAFETY PRECAUTIONS

Wear protective gloves (latex or plastic) and long sleeves. If mold is present, wear a respirator. Some mold species are toxic; if any health effects are observed, contact a doctor and/or mycologist. When cleaning items with dry mold, make sure there is adequate ventilation that draws the mold spores away from you, e.g., a vacuum cleaner. Wash your hands after handling materials with mold.

AIR-DRYING

Absorb excess moisture using a clean sponge, paper, or bath towels, etc. Do not blot on hand-written ink or fragile surfaces. Do not use printed newsprint for blotting; ink can transfer. Use fans to provide maximum air circulation but do not aim fans directly at the drying materials.

AIR-DRYING PAPER DOCUMENTS, MAPS, POSTERS, ETC.

Paper is very fragile when wet and must be handled with care. Provide adequate support. Blot excess water off the documents.

Do not attempt to separate individual items while very wet. You may leave them in stacks no higher than ?" to dry. If pages can be separated safely, they can be interleaved using absorbent or separating materials (e.g., wax paper). Change interleaving materials until item is dry.

Clean, unrusted window screens, stacked with bricks or wood blocks between them, will provide a drying surface with maximum air circulation. If drying items on a hard surface, cover the area with absorbent materials and change when wet.

When items are almost dry, place them between protective sheets such as unprinted newsprint and put a light weight on them to flatten. (If the item is too wet when placed under weights, you may create a microenvironment for mold.)

AIR-DRYING FRAMED ITEMS

Place the frame glass-side down and remove the backing materials.

Carefully remove object and air-dry. If the object is stuck to the glass, do not remove; instead dry frame with object inside, glass-side down on a flat surface.

AIR-DRYING BOOKS

Fan books open and stand on top or bottom edge; never stand them on the front edge. Stand books on driest edge first to provide support. As the book dries, turn it upside-down to the opposite edge every few hours.

Place a sheet of wax paper larger than the pages between the front and back cover and adjacent page before standing on edges. Replace the interleaving as it becomes saturated.

When the book is no longer wet, but still cool to the touch, close and place on a solid surface with a slight weight to keep distortion to a minimum. Check frequently to ensure that no mold is growing.

RECOVERY OF WATER-DAMAGED COLLECTIONS WITH MOLD

Active mold looks either fuzzy or slimy. Do not attempt to remove active mold. Dormant mold is dry and powdery. See safety procedures above for handling mold.

Stop mold outbreaks by improving environmental conditions. Humidity levels should be as low as possible below 75 percent. Use a dehumidifier. Low temperatures—below 68° F.—are recommended.

Short exposure to sunlight and circulating air outdoors may help to dry moldy items more rapidly. (There may be light damage; use this treatment only with materials where damage is acceptable.)

When the mold has become dormant through drying it can be removed, using a vacuum cleaner and/or a soft brush. After vacuuming, dispose of bag. Clean brushes to prevent spreading the mold spores. Safety precautions are particularly important in this stage.

Water damage to materials may be irreversible. The treatment of items of high monetary, historic, or sentimental value should be referred to a conservator. The Foundation of American Institute for Conservation (FAIC) maintains a referral service of conservators who will be able to provide more information about treatment of items in private collections. Contact the FAIC office: FAIC, 1717 K. Street, N.W., Suite 301, Washington, D.C. 20006. Provide a complete description of the object you wish to have treated, the type of conservation service you require, the geographic area in which you prefer to have the work done, and your regular mailing address.

[*Whole Library Handbook 3*, by George M. Eberhart. Reproduced with permission.]

15

Collection Development

The books and other materials on your branch's shelves—your collection—are resources to be constantly tended. They are the library's wealth, and your responsibility.

Ordering

Ask the collection development department for their policies regarding ordering materials for your library system. Know what your community needs and wants. If your library system has centralized ordering let that department know what you need. Base your order requests on user surveys, a suggestion box, patron requests, and circulation patterns. If you do your own ordering, use the same criteria. Never base your order selections completely on personal interests or prejudices.

Weeding

Why weed? Why remove any book from the library's collection? For several reasons. One very obvious reason is space. As you continue to acquire new books and materials, you will run out of room on your shelves if none are weeded. It is expensive to maintain books on your shelves that are not used. Also, it is hard to find what you want on the shelves when they are packed tightly. Some librarians find it difficult to weed their collections. They just can't bring themselves to withdraw a book that someone may want to read someday. Books are sacred to every library's collection, but if a book is falling apart and is not a good candidate for circulating anymore, it should be weeded. If that title is essential to your collection you can always order another if it is still in print, or something newer that is comparable. Weeding should not be an internal struggle, it should be viewed as a way to clear your stacks to make them more attractive and to make your collection more accessible.

Keep your collection current. Know your library's policy on weeding. Weed outdated books and order new editions. Your library should not be a warehouse for books. It should be a usable collection of up-to-date information.

Weed all books that are tattered. No one wants to borrow books or materials that are torn and look tattered. Order new copies if possible. Try to rid your shelves of anything that looks like it should be discarded. I have seen branch managers keep tattered books on the shelves because they don't have another book on that subject. Something on the shelf is not always better than nothing. If a book is discarded and a patron needs it afterward, try to either reserve one from another branch or acquire an interlibrary loan until you can reorder it. Better yet, try to find them a newer title on the same subject. There are many books that go into detail on weeding various areas of the library collection. Make sure that you are weeding based on condition, age, whether it has been superseded by another edition, or other factors. Talk to your boss to see if there are any specific guidelines that you should follow.

Factors Discouraging Weeding of Your Collection

Too much emphasis is placed on the number of books in your collection. A library is not a warehouse for books. It should be a collection of items that are attractive, meet the needs of your community, and are easily accessible. If your boss demands that you weed regularly and you also have many other demands, it may be a source of stress for you. You might feel that your time is better spent doing other things. If you as a manager don't believe in discarding books, your collection will soon need an extensive weeding. Libraries that have not weeded in three years or more will find that when they do weed, it will be an enormous task. If you have problems with patrons or staff stealing or defacing books that will no longer be available, you may not want to add to that collection of unavailable items by weeding. Books that are mis-shelved may as well have been weeded because they are also lost to the collection. You might find yourself torn between what you feel people want to read and what you and various sources determine to be good books. Don't be afraid to weed your collection. Studies have shown that after weeding

1. Your overall circulation statistics should increase.

2. Patrons find what they need faster because they don't have as many books to search through.

3. The accuracy of your shelving should increase because while weeding you are also shelf reading.

Criteria for Weeding a Branch Library's Collection

1. Books that are in poor physical condition. If you would not want to read it because of its physical condition, chances are that patrons won't want to either.

2. The information in the book is obsolete. Old computer programs, financial advice, laws, and politics, for example, go out of date more quickly than other titles.

3. The content of the book is no longer valuable. It may be sexist, racist, or reflecting conditions that have changed.

4. It is written in a language not used in your community.

5. Age. Many nonfiction books have specific spans of time where they are most useful. Some of these are travel guides, textbooks, and medical guides. Check with your collection development department for guidance on how many years you should keep these kind of books.

6. Books that should never have been purchased because of inaccuracies and poorly written content.

7. Circulation history. If a title has not circulated within an extended time period set by your library system, it should be weeded. There is no reason to keep a nonfiction book on your shelf that has not circulated in five years. Of course this rule does not apply to books that normally do not circulate, such as reference books.

Periodicals and Serials

Weed items that are not indexed. If you have an incomplete set and cannot order a replacement for the missing volumes, the set should be discarded. If you have a serial that has ceased publication, it needs to be weeded. If not, you will have patrons asking for the newer editions.

Criteria for Keeping Materials

1. If the books and materials continue to circulate on a regular basis, keep them unless their condition is poor. In that case, replace if possible.

2. If the title is listed in a standard catalog as part of a library's core collection, it should be kept.

3. New books should be kept at least one year regardless of their circulation history.

4. Keep all unabridged, biographical, and subject dictionaries.

The bottom line is to follow the collection development department's weeding policy for your library system. Weed regularly on an ongoing basis and your collection will be one that is both used and appreciated by your community.

Request for Reconsideration

Find out your library system's procedure for patrons to challenge books in your collection. The patron should be allowed to complete a Reconsideration of Materials form. A committee will read the book and meet to talk about what action should be taken. The committee will discuss the item and any passages or information that the patron finds offensive in the work. They will check the collection to see if there is a balance in representing all points of view. For example, if a patron is complaining about a title because it represents single-parent families, the committee should look at the titles in the library's collection to see what other titles are there that represent the traditional nuclear family. The director of the library will probably be the person who sends a letter to the patron telling them what action will be taken. Your policy will dictate whether or not the item is removed from the shelves until a decision is made. See "Banned Books Week" in Chapter XIX, "Programming," and Appendixes A and D.

Best-Seller Lists

Make sure that you display the current *New York Times* best-seller's lists (hardback, paperback, fiction, non-fiction, children's) in your library. Patrons are interested in what everyone else is reading and all titles on the fiction list will probably have reserves on them. If you notice patrons borrowing books by authors who have new books on the best-seller list, ask if they would like to place their names on the reserve list for the author's new book. They may not have realized that the author has a new book.

Special Areas

The way your materials are displayed may determine the rate at which they circulate. If it is difficult for people to find items, the likelihood of their being borrowed is decreased. Patrons should not have to ask for directions to the most frequently checked out items. New books, audiovisual materials, and paperbacks should be within view of the circulation desk.

Paperbacks

Paperbacks have about a two-year circulation life. After that, they start to look worn, are outdated, and should be replaced. Genre labels should be taped on the spine of the books to help patrons find their favorites. Children's series titles should be shelved together on racks by title to make it easier to find titles from the series that they have not yet read.

Young Adult

Young adult books tend to circulate slowly. You can decide if you want to shelve these books as a separate collection or with the adult collection. Many teens do not borrow from the young adult collection because they feel that they are adults and they want to get books from the adult collection. Make decisions based on space and patron usage.

Foreign-Language Materials

Survey your community to determine how many volumes of foreign-language materials your library needs to own. If you have a significant percentage of Spanish-speaking or other non–English-speaking patrons in your community, you need to order a variety of materials to meet their needs. Include both adult and juvenile materials. Have materials in your collection translated into Spanish, French, German, Italian, Japanese, and Chinese. Order materials in any language that is spoken in your community. Patrons who visit your library from foreign countries have the right to be able to read something in their native language. Don't have the attitude that international patrons should all learn English. Many English speakers visit foreign countries without being fluent in the language of the country that they are visiting.

Large-Print Books

Large-print books should be placed on eye-level or lower shelving. Many seniors read large-print books and they can't see the titles if the books are above their heads. Make sure that you continue to update this collection if you have a large readership.

Oversized/Undersized Books

Oversized and undersized books can be a real problem to shelve. Books should be and were made to be shelved with their spines facing you. Books should not be turned down to fit in the shelves. If they stick out, however, you can't read neighboring titles. If your shelves can be adjusted to accommodate those books, do it. If not, buy special shelving, an adjustable bookcase, or some other unit to house the oversized and undersized books. If you move those books to another area, make sure you indicate in the computer where they are located. Tiny undersized children's books can be placed in a basket in a corner where the children can help themselves. Undersized adult books should stay with the rest of the collection unless you have a special place in your library where they would be readily accessible. Try not to have books in too many different places. Patrons are easily frustrated and will get upset if a book is not where the computer says it is.

Paperback Exchange

Many patrons donate books to libraries on a regular basis. They especially love to donate paperbacks. You may find yourself with boxes of small paperback books in great condition. If you have a lot of patrons that read paperbacks and you want to circulate them without sending them to the main library to be processed, you can start a paperback exchange. Stamp your branch name on them if you want to and either place them in a rack or shelve them with a sign nearby. Let patrons know that they don't need a library card to check them out and they can borrow as many as they like. They can bring one from home in exchange for the one they checked out or just return the ones that they borrowed. It is a good alternative for patrons who have problems getting a library card but want to check something out. Also, people vacationing can use the library and be able to take paperbacks home to read without getting a library card.

If your library is automated, you will have to record the total number circulated manually and add those totals to your monthly statistics. Since the paperback exchange titles were not purchased by the library, I don't charge late fees or replacement costs for lost books. When they are checked out I tell patrons to return them whenever they are finished reading them.

Of course, if you receive a paperback edition of a bestseller or a book with reserves on it, you will want to send it to the cataloging department to be added to your collection.

Finding/Filling Gaps in the Collection

Knowing what you have in your collection may be easy to determine. Browsing the shelves, seeing what books and materials are returned, and looking at the new books coming in from the cataloging department are all ways to know what you own. Finding out what you don't have and where the gaps are will take more investigating. Listen to your patrons and hear what they are asking for. Look at books coming in as reserves. Check your interlibrary loan request applications. These are all indications that patrons want items that are not available at your branch. Keep a small notebook at each service desk to record subjects that are missing from your collection. If you have areas of your collection where all of the titles are outdated, there is a gap in that area of the collection because none of those titles are current. Try to have something on as many subjects as possible.

Genre Stickers

Make your collection more user friendly by attaching genre (thrillers, science fiction, mystery, historical fiction) stickers to the spines of your fiction books. Patrons looking for books in specific genres will see at a glance which ones they are. This is especially helpful if you work at a busy branch or have a staff shortage. Patrons can help themselves without asking for assistance in finding books of a specific genre. Make sure that you label the books with the correct genre sticker. Get confirmation from the book itself, the bibliographic record in the computer, or another reliable source. Post a sign with a sample of each sticker and what it represents. If you don't have printed stickers you may use colorful dots. Assign each genre a specific colored dot. Post a sign with a sample of each dot and the genre it represents.

Labeling Books Belonging to Your Branch

If you have a problem with books from other branches being shelved in your collection, you could undertake a project that is tedious but well worth the effort. Divide your collection into sections, assigning all employees the same number of sections. Make sure that everyone has some of each designation. For example, each person should have some juvenile, some fiction, some nonfiction, etc. As each person goes through his assigned sections, he should open each book to make sure that the book belongs to your branch. If it does, attach a piece of colored tape to the spine of the book. This tape can be purchased in various widths, strengths, and colors. I chose a half-inch-wide yellow tape that could easily be cut. Cut off enough tape to fit around the spine of the book without sticking to the book next to it and apply the tape to the spine.

Make sure that all the books have tape placed the same distance from the top edge of the book so that, when the books are shelved, they all look uniform.

Although this is a tedious process, when books are returned you know immediately which ones belong to your library and which ones don't. You won't believe, until you try it, how much easier it is to keep track of your books. Your books won't end up on other branch shelves because of the tape. If the entire library system adopts the idea, each branch could be assigned its own color of labeling tape.

Library pages that don't bother to open each book to see which branch they belong to will know which ones are yours and which ones belong to another branch. If the tape doesn't stay on because of the books being shelved and reshelved, you may have to put clear adhesive tape over each strip of colored tape to hold it secure.

Computer Reports

In order to keep your collection clutter-free, every few years you should obtain computerized reports on the status of books and materials that are not circulating on a regular basis. This will help you make decisions when weeding and locating gaps in your collection. Below are a few reports that you might want to request from your systems manager or computer operator. Think about other reports that may help you in your collection development.

1. **Dusty book report**. This is a listing of books that have not circulated in several years. You may want to go back two years or more. You and your systems administrator can talk about an appropriate time frame. If you have a list of books that have not circulated for three years, do you really want them sitting on your shelves taking up space? Make sure that you disregard any title on your list that cannot circulate. These will include your reference books.

2. **Claims returned**. These are materials on patron accounts that are reported as being returned. Many books that are claimed returned are found on the shelves. If these materials can be found and cleared from patron accounts, it will enhance your level of customer satisfaction. This report should be requested monthly if possible.

3. **Missing Report**. This report lists books and materials marked as "missing" in the computer. Sometimes you can search for a book for days and not find it. You mark it missing in the computer so that patrons will know that it is unavailable. Then all of a sudden the book turns up again. It could have been taken by a patron for a period of time then returned. It could have slipped behind a shelf, been given to a patron without being checked out, or shelved in a completely different area of the library. If you have a Missing Report, you can periodically search for these materials and clear their status in the computer. Your library pages won't tell you every time they find a book misshelved, especially as it is their job to make sure all items are shelved correctly. Sometimes your staff may borrow books and take them home without checking them out. You may find a book that you were searching for on someone's desk. The Missing Report will tell you what to look for.

Printed AV Lists

Although your audiovisual materials may be listed in your library's computerized card catalog, patrons like to see a printed list of the items you own at your library. Enter your videocassettes, DVDs, books on compact disk, books on audiotape, music CDs, etc., into individual databases on your personal computer. Sort them by title and subject. Place the printed lists in separate binders. Update your lists as you receive new audiovisual materials. Always have a list of the newest titles received. You could make a list of the current titles each month. Post a sign near the audiovisuals with the newest titles listed separately.

Music CDs

Music on compact disks could be a shelving problem if you don't have a unit to house them at your branch. Almost all of them will have a call number in the 780s. Trying to place them in shelflist order and keeping them in order can be a nightmare. I find that it works better if they are shelved by genre. For example, have a section of your display case or shelves marked "Jazz" and place a label marked "Jazz" on each disk cover. Label another section "Classical" and place a label marked "Classical" on the front of each cover. Then sort the cases alphabetically by artist or composer, as appropriate. It will be much easier to shelve them and keep them in order by genre and it will be easier for patrons to find what they want. Most patrons have specific interests and like to browse in those areas. Also, if patrons are looking for a specific title and know what type of music it is, they could just look in that section rather than looking through all of the compact disks. Have your library pages shelf read that area regularly to make sure all disks are where they should be.

Shifting the Collection

When your bookshelves are almost full and you have problems shelving returned books, you must shift the collection. I like to have about 12 inches of space at the end of each shelf if possible. Try not to shelve books on the very top shelf high above patron's heads or on the very bottom where no one can see the titles unless they get down on the floor. Before you do any shifting, make sure that the books on the shelves you are shifting are in correct shelflist order. Don't shift any book that is obviously ready to be discarded. Shifting should not begin until weeding and shelf reading ends.

Make sure that the person doing the shifting knows the procedure. Take a group of books from the right end of one shelf and place them at the beginning of the next shelf. If you keep going you will end up with the collection being shifted. Make sure all shifted shelves have bookends; you don't want books falling on patrons or staff members. Look at the entire collection that you are weeding and shifting. Make sure that you have room to move. You don't want to shift all the way to the end and discover that you have one shelf left with three shelves worth of books to be shifted. If you weed your duplicate copies and they are in good condition, ask the other branch managers if they need them in their collections.

16

Service Desks

Make sure that each service desk has ample staff coverage. Always have at least two people at the desk; if one person has to leave to help a patron, another staff member is there to help. Never have a situation where a patron is standing at the desk waiting to be helped and staff are visible to them but are busy doing other things and not noticing them standing there.

Make sure all staff know everything that is going on at the branch: upcoming programs, workshops, meetings, etc. When patrons call to ask about programs, everyone should know what they are, when they are, and what they are about.

The Key Word Is "Service"

Service desks are points of contact with your patrons. These desks include the reference desk, circulation desk, children's desk, young adult desk, reader's advisory and any area in the library where a patron goes to receive information from staff. The way these desks are run can determine whether your branch thrives or just exists. The way your patrons are served is one of the most important aspects of library service. Make sure that all of your staff realize how important working at the service desk is. It all begins with the interaction between your staff and the patron. The following are several points that are essential for good customer service, increased circulation, and patron retention.

1. **Smile**. A pleasant face is very approachable. Patrons feel more at ease asking questions and visiting your branch if the staff are friendly.

2. **Learn your patrons' names if possible**. If you don't know their names, when you receive their library card or some form of identification, make sure that you call them by name: "Have a good day, Mr. Smith."

3. **Refer to patrons as "sir" or "ma'am."** Never answer "Yeah" or "Uh-huh," always "Yes sir" or "No ma'am." This shows respect and is very professional.

4. **Help patrons locate materials**. Don't just point and say, "It's over there." If you are busy with other patrons, give the questioner as much detail about the location of the materials as possible and tell them that you will help them as soon as you can. When you are free, go over and ask if they found what they were looking for. If a patron says that he checked the shelf but couldn't find the book, offer to help. Don't say, "If it's not on the shelf it must be checked out." Go over to the shelf and look. Many times patrons are looking in the wrong area. They may not understand the call number system. The book may be on display or in the new-books section. Help the patron as much as you would help a friend or family member.

5. **Don't give patrons special privileges**. When you do that, other patrons waiting in line will expect you to do the same for them and their friends. This is not the same as compromising when a patron has a problem with their library record. A special privilege is when you completely disregard the policy. This includes putting favorite patrons first on the reserve list when others are waiting or allowing them to keep books and other materials out past the due date and not charging them overdue fees. All patrons should be treated the same way. Don't abuse your authority.

6. **Never make verbal judgments** about materials that patrons check out or ask for. If a patron is obviously doing her child's homework, make no comment. You should only provide the assistance and information that she needs. Our job is to provide information, not to make judgments. If a patron borrows materials that may be objectionable to you personally, don't make any comments about the material. What patrons borrow is none of our business.

Customer Service

Try to satisfy every patron if at all possible. You may have to compromise or just take the patron's word for it. The computer is not always the final authority. Do some checking. Just because the computer shows that the patron did not return a book, don't argue with them. Check the shelves. It is better to check the shelves in the beginning than to insist that the computer is right and then find the book in the library.

Here are some customer service tips:

- Give your patrons quality service at all times.

- Always thank the patron and wish them a good day.

- Always ask if you can help whether someone comes to you or not. If you notice a patron wandering around, ask if you can help them find something. Many patrons are afraid to come to the desk to ask a question. They don't ask because they think that their question is silly.

- Be energetic and have a positive attitude.

- When a patron calls and asks a question, restate the question to be sure that you understood them correctly. Ask the patron for their name and telephone number if the question will take longer than a few minutes to answer. Don't leave patrons on hold for more than a minute or so.

- You should care whether or not a patron finds what they are looking for. If what they need is not there, offer to see if another branch might have it. Do whatever you can to find what they need. Even if the item is not located anywhere in the library system the patron will appreciate the effort that you went through to try to find it. Go the extra mile.

- Solve patron problems quickly. Don't leave discrepancies riding on their library record forever. Ask the patron to pay whatever they owe, or compromise with them, or clear the record. If they know about their fines and want to pay in installments, allow them to do that. Don't have a situation where every time a patron comes in to borrow materials, someone reminds them of a book that is on their record that is checked out to them but they claim to have returned. If there is a problem and you are clearing the record, let the patron know that. Don't just stand in front of your computer pressing buttons; tell the patron that you are waiving their fines or clearing that lost book.

- Explain policies to patrons in lay terms. Most patrons don't know the library jargon that we use and they might think something is negative when actually it is positive.

- Remember not to be so preoccupied that you don't notice a patron standing at the desk.

- Call patrons back. If there is a patron who you know has been waiting anxiously for a book, give them a call when the book arrives and let them know that their book is in.

- Thank patrons for waiting.

THE TEN COMMANDMENTS OF LIBRARY SERVICE

1. Patrons are the most important people in our library.

2. Patrons are not outsiders. They are owners of our library.

3. Patrons are not an interruption of our work. They are the purpose of it.

4. Patrons do us a favor when they call. We are not doing them a favor when we serve them.

5. Patrons are not cold statistics. They are human beings with feelings and emotions like our own.

6. Patrons are not people with whom we argue or match wits.

7. Patrons are people who bring us their wants. It is our job to fill those wants.

8. Patrons are deserving of the most courteous and attentive treatment we can give them.

9. Patrons are not dependent on us. We are dependent on them.

10. Patrons are the lifeblood of our library.

[Borrowed from Libby Collins, Sara Hightower Regional Library,...] Rome, GA

DOS AND DON'TS AT THE SERVICE DESK

Do insist on proper telephone etiquette from your staff. They should say good morning or good afternoon, the name of your branch, and identify themselves as the person speaking. "Good morning. Columbia Public Library, Laura speaking. May I help you?" Make sure everyone's voice is upbeat and they have smiles in their voices. Don't make your patrons feel as though they called at a bad time or that they are bothering you. Also, if you need to transfer the call to another department, tell the patron that you will be glad to transfer their call. Don't just transfer them so all they hear is the sound of being connected somewhere else. Tell them that you are connecting them to the children's department, for example.

Do make sure that you work at the service desk yourself as often as possible. The manager needs to be visible to the public so that he/she knows the community and their needs. The public needs to know who you are and to develop a working relationship with you. Your staff also needs to see that you don't stay in your office all day but that you work the service desk just as they do. How can you supervise and give direction to your staff if you are not on the front lines yourself?

Do provide good customer service, always. This cannot be emphasized enough. Don't allow a bad day or a bad mood to affect your ability to courteously serve your patrons.

Do remind your staff that during busy times of the year patrons become more irritable. During the summer when their children are home all day, parents become more impatient. Expect it. It is easier to deal with if you do.

Don't talk about patrons when you are at the service desk. Other patrons in the library probably know them and it is just not good public relations.

Don't complain about your job or your boss to patrons. If you are not happy with your job, find another one. Patrons don't want to hear you complain about working in a place where they may need to ask for your assistance.

Don't have personal conversations at the service desk. Voices carry to all areas of the library even when you speak in a low tone.

Don't make your patrons feel stupid. Don't say, "The computer has simple instructions on it. You shouldn't have any problems." Instead say that there are instructions on or near the computer but if they have any questions let you know and you will be happy to help.

Maps to Branches

Everyone in your branch needs to know where all the other branches in the library system are located. This is especially important for those on your staff who answer the telephone. Patrons want clear, simple directions to your branch and to all others. Place maps printed with clear directions near telephones for staff to refer to. Don't ask patrons to call other branches to get directions to their locations. If you called a department store to inquire about the availability of an item and they told you that they did not have it but their other store did, how would you feel if the salesperson told you to call the other store for directions to it?

Genealogy

Many patrons are interested in their family history. It is a good idea to have a collection of local history information in your branch. If your main library has a large collection of genealogy materials, you could refer patrons to main for further study. Always have local histories of your city in both your reference and circulating collections. Maintain a list of sources available from your main library on genealogy. Maintain a vertical file with newspaper clippings and other information about the community that you serve.

City Directories

Personal information, like patron's addresses and telephone numbers, should not be given over the telephone. When patrons call to ask for someone else's name or telephone number from the telephone book or city directory, politely explain that you would be invading that person's privacy if you reported that information. If a female patron called and said that she found a telephone number in her husband's shirt pocket and wanted to see to whom it belonged by having you look in the city directory, would you feel comfortable? It is much better for the patron seeking such information to come in and do her own detective work. That way, neither you nor your staff will be involved in any misunderstandings between patrons.

If your library system's policy is to give personal information from directories over the telephone, be careful how you disseminate that information. For example, if someone asks you to look up a telephone number of another patron in the city directory, you need to tell him or her what source you are using and the date of that source. That way if the telephone number is incorrect you have given the source of your information.

Never give a patron information taken from someone's library record! If two patrons are parent and child and the child is an adult, the parent has no right to ask to know what the child has checked out or what fines are owed to the library.

Reference Desk

The reference or information desk is where most of the research questions will be answered. Make sure the reference desk or its vicinity has the necessary supplies and books needed to serve your patrons effectively. Keep your most asked-for items at the desk so staff won't have to leave the desk each time a patron asks to borrow something. Below is a list of items that you may want to keep at the information desk.

1. Scratch paper.
2. Writing instruments.
3. Correcting fluid.
4. Magnifying glass.
5. Calculator.
6. Question/Answer pads to record questions from patrons and the answers that were found.
7. Contact numbers for the administrative staff.
8. Supplies for machines. This includes toner and paper.
9. Stapler.
10. Scotch tape.
11. Statistical counter for recording reference statistics.
12. Floppy disks for sale.
13. Reference policy.
14. Ready-reference collection.
15. Pencil sharpener.
16. Book cart for books to be reshelved.
17. Step stools.
18. Vertical file of local information.

Circulation Desk

The circulation desk is usually the first and last stop patrons make when they use your branch. This is where they register for library cards, check books in and out, and pay fines. Keep a copy of the circulation policy and procedures at the desk for staff to refer to. Always check the date-due cards each morning to make sure that they have the correct date stamped on them.

Decide how you want to handle returned items. If they are sorted right after they are discharged and placed on book carts, your library pages can take a cart to the shelves and begin shelving without having to sort them. If no library pages are available, the books could be placed on sorting shelves within their genres until they can be shelved.

Unclaimed Items

Unclaimed items, or items requested but not picked up by patrons from the service desk, should not be allowed to stay out of the collection past their pick-up date. When others are waiting for items on hold, unclaimed items should be processed immediately to go to the next person on the list. Unless a patron calls and asks for an item to be held a day or two longer, materials should be placed either in circulation or back on the shelves. When patrons are waiting for their requests, try to fill those requests as soon as possible.

Telephone Renewals

If your library system allows patrons to renew items by telephone, make sure your staff is trained in all the procedures required to make the transaction flow smoothly. Decide what types of identification you will require from the patron. Will you ask for their library card number? The barcode number from the book? Just their name? Make sure, if you renew by using their name, that you check their address, telephone number, or the title of one of the books against their record to be sure you have the correct patron. After renewing, tell the patron what their new due date is. If an item cannot be renewed for any reason, let the patron know that they still have the original due date. If a patron calls and wants several items renewed and the service desk is busy, look up their library record and print it out, noting those items the patron wants renewed, and tell them that you will call back with the new due dates. Be sure to ask for the telephone number just in case the number that you have on file has been changed. When it is less busy, renew the items and call the patron back with the new due dates.

Children's Desk

The children's department should be very cheerful with low book displays, stuffed animals, small tables and chairs, and beanbags if possible. Accessible board books for toddlers and areas for storytimes make this department very inviting.

Unattended Children

At one time or another you will have an unattended child. They may have been dropped off or brought by a school bus, or be waiting for a ride after your branch closes. Know what your library system's policy is regarding unattended children. Post a copy of the policy in a prominent place in your library. Do not take a child home. Although you may feel you are doing the child and parent a favor, you are putting yourself and your child at risk. If you have an automobile accident while the child is in your care you could be liable. Also, you don't want to be accused of inappropriate behavior when you are alone with the child. If the library has closed and you have a child who does not have a ride home, call the police to escort the child home. If you don't want to do that, have two staff members wait with the child until an adult comes to pick him or her up. Give the adult a copy of the unattended-child policy. If you have problems with the same child being left unattended on a regular basis, let the administration know so that they can follow up with the patron with a formal letter or telephone call.

Recommended Books for Children

Parents often ask for lists of recommended titles for their children. There are many sources of titles from which you can create bookmarks and bibliographies to distribute. You can choose Caldecott, Newbery, Coretta Scott King, Junior, and Young Adult book award winners. Have separate bookmarks for each grade level. Your main library's children's department may have created reading lists recommended by their children's librarian. The titles of the books, a short synopsis of each one, and their locations in the collection will help parents and children find books they want to read.

Accelerated Reading Lists

Many elementary schools require their students to read books from an accelerated reader list, each book earning points for its readers. After the student has read a book, they take a computerized test on their knowledge of the book. Their score on the test determines the number of points they receive for the book. A perfect score gives the student the full number of points associated with that title. Ask each elementary school in your area if they have accelerated reader lists. If they do, ask for a copy of the list. Keep each school's list in a separate binder with their name on the outside. Parents expect to find those lists at the library. If you only have one school in your area you could separate those books on the shelves or place colored dots on the spines to make them easier to find.

17

Patrons with Special Needs

Homeschoolers

More and more parents have made the decision to teach their children at home. Homeschooling organizations are getting larger and more diverse each year. Homeschooling families depend heavily upon libraries to support their curriculums. Reach out to home schooling groups. Offer your meeting rooms for their events. Give tours of the library and purchase materials to meet their specific goals. Ask homeschooling parents what the library can do for them. Create brochures and bibliographies specifically for homeschoolers. Include books and audiovisual materials available at your library that they might be interested in. Make the names and addresses of local and national homeschooling organizations available. Develop a packet to distribute to new homeschooling families with resources offered by the library, Internet websites, and programming. Read books on homeschooling for librarians. The books will give you details on specific programs and events that can be held at your branch to support homeschoolers and their families.

Homeschooling families heavily use and support libraries. They want and expect many things from libraries, which include:

1. Space. It is a frequently mentioned need—meeting rooms, study rooms, use of whatever space is possible to obtain at zero or very low cost. Homeschoolers often engage in cooperative learning activities and would very much appreciate the opportunity to use library space.

2. Family-oriented programs and activities are often preferred by homeschoolers, rather than grade-level or age-level based. The homeschooled kids are used to working in multi-age environments and they are comfortable that way. This is more convenient for parents, and is more "natural" and allows older children to lend a hand or serve as role models for the younger ones. Libraries can find out from the homeschoolers in their area whether or not there are specific activities or programs that

they would like to participate in during the day. These might range from family read-aloud times to book discussion clubs for teens.

3. Volunteer opportunities for homeschooling families to provide services to the library itself can be provided. Some libraries have age limits for volunteer work, but if they are willing to waive those age limits, homeschooling families can be a great resource and parents can supervise younger children's work.

4. Access to technology such as Internet services or other computer-based resources, and the ability to use or borrow software such as educational games is appreciated by many homeschoolers. Although many homeschoolers have extensive computer resources in their own homes, there are also many who can't afford computers and Internet connections and educational software.

5. Support for academic needs as well as leisure reading is of interest to homeschoolers. This requires librarians to become informed about the types of learning resources or curriculum used by homeschoolers in their area and to determine what kinds of juvenile and young adult fiction and nonfiction materials would best serve their needs.

6. Video and audiotapes, DVDs, and compact disks are frequently used by many homeschoolers. Many homeschoolers would be interested in tapes of PBS or other educational programs or instructional videos as well as high quality unabridged books on tape.

7. Extended borrowing periods and allowing families to check out more materials at one time can be very helpful to homeschooling families.

8. Homeschooling information can be offered by libraries, by providing folders or notebooks with information about state laws and names and addresses of homeschooling organizations in the area. Resources specifically to help those just considering or beginning homeschooling are often needed.

9. State educational standards, courses of study, or curriculum guides can be made available in library reference sections.

10. Bibliographic information has been collected by some libraries to help homeschoolers find information when they are studying a specific subject.

11. Display space for homeschoolers to display art or science projects could be provided.

12. Science equipment could be provided on loan to home schooling families.

13. Access to college and career information would be appreciated by home schooling teens.

14. Library tours and information on the various library collections and any special services would be of interest to most home-schooling families.

15. Speakers on topics of interest to homeschooling parents could be arranged by libraries. These might include, for example, speakers on child development, learning theories, or lectures on specific academic subjects. Talks by experienced homeschoolers on subjects related specifically to homeschooling would also be appreciated.

[*Whole Library Handbook 2*, by George Eberhart. Reproduced with permission.]

Some libraries have had problems with some homeschooling groups. The groups have been very demanding, borrow everything that you have on a particular topic, expect special privileges, and can be noisy when many groups visit at once. It will be part of your job to balance the needs of homeschoolers against those of your branch's other patrons.

Spanish-Speaking Patrons

Many libraries are in communities where the Hispanic population has risen significantly in recent years. As our community changes so does our need to develop new programs and acquire new materials to serve all of our users. There are many things that can be done at your branch to increase usage of your library by Spanish-speaking patrons.

1. Offer ESL (English as a Second Language) classes at your branch. Contact the Literacy Association in your area to have your branch listed as a location for free classes.

2. Order bilingual signs for your branch or print them from your computer. You will need signs that announce programming, services, websites, new titles in Spanish, and library hours.

3. Place materials in Spanish in an area where patrons can find them easily, not in the back of the library where no one knows that they are there.

4. Recruit volunteers to conduct storytimes and adult programs in Spanish.

5. Order new books, periodicals, and AV materials for your branch in Spanish.

6. Do outreach programming at Spanish-speaking classes in the schools.

7. Ask a Spanish-speaking volunteer to teach your staff some basic words in Spanish in order to help patrons that do not speak English.

Homeless Patrons

Almost every library has at least one homeless person who comes in regularly. Not every homeless person is easily recognizable, however. The homeless include women, children, the elderly, and people of all cultures. Homeless people are a part of your community and your branch should strive to meet their needs. They should not be labeled as homeless by staff and avoided. Many homeless people would like the opportunity to get back on their feet. The library is the perfect place for them to begin gathering information. Make available information packets that include social service agencies, employment offices, and housing. Place your current newspapers and periodicals in a comfortable area. If possible, have cushioned chairs or sofas.

Plan programs geared to the needs of the homeless population. Don't ask patrons if they are homeless, however. Plan your programs, post signage, and hopefully the people who need the services will attend. Plan programs with speakers from various organizations to talk about their services and how people can get help. Plan a free health fair. Serve refreshments at all of your programs and say so on your signage. If you receive a lot of donated books, consider giving some to a homeless shelter in your area.

Problem Patrons

Any library patron can become a problem patron when she is overcome by a situation. This can take the form of angry demands, loud protestations, and even threats of violence.

When dealing with a problem patron, smile and say hello. For example, "Hello, I'm Mrs. Rivers, the branch manager. May I help you?" Listen to everything the patron has to say without interrupting. When they have said everything they wanted to say then you should respond. Remain as calm as you can. Give the patron eye contact and sympathize with their problem. State the policy and try to compromise while staying within the guidelines of the library's policies. Don't completely disregard the policy just to get rid of the patron but do have an open mind and give the patron the benefit of the doubt. We do want to make our patrons happy but at the same time they need to know what our policies are. Sometimes you may have to waive fines or take a book off a patron's record if they insist that they returned it. It's not worth losing a patron over a book that may really have been returned.

Tell the patron that you want to help. Be as flexible as you can. If your library system allows you to compromise, the patron will be happier and so will you because you both will win. For example, if their overdue fines are $10 and the patron says that they thought that the video tapes were 5 cents per day instead of $1 per day maybe you can compromise and ask them to pay half the amount owed. That way you can recover some of the fees and the patron does not have to pay the full amount. It is a win-win solution. Always tell the patron what you can do when there is a situation where you can't do what they want. If they request something that is against the policy just say, "No, I'm sorry I can't do that, but I can…." Always try to have a positive alternative for the patron.

Angry Patrons

When you notice a patron who is speaking loudly and is very angry, you must take control of the situation immediately. Don't wait for a staff member to call you because they may not be able to leave the desk. Go to the service desk and identify yourself. Listen and remain calm. Maintain a comfortable distance from the patron but under no circumstances are you to touch the patron. Tell him what you are willing to do to solve the problem; don't allow an argument to develop. If the patron continues to yell, ask them to step away from the desk where you can talk in private. As long as they continue to talk about the problem, be willing to help. If they verbally abuse you or your staff, make it clear that you can't help them unless they calm down.

If you see that the situation is escalating or you fear for your safety, leave the service desk and call the police. They are trained to handle people who are verbally and physically abusive. Call your boss after notifying the police to let him or her know what happened. Just walk away from the patron and wait for the police to arrive.

Be alert to repeat offenders and abusers of the library system—those who try to have every fine waived, for example. Waiving fines should not be the norm; it should only happen when you feel that patrons could indeed have either paid a fine or returned a book as they say. Believe them. Good public relations go a long way.

Attend workshops on problem patrons. Have meetings with your staff on how to handle problem patrons. There is a very good book called *Small Libraries*, by Sally Gardner Reed, that goes into more detail about handling problem patrons.

18

Your Community

Your branch is part of the neighborhood, but it is also part of the larger community. Research and do a community analysis. There are many sources in libraries and on the Internet to tell you what it should include. Study this overview of your community and its residents. It helps with planning programs and collection development.

Contact community leaders. Speak to school groups, church groups, etc. Let them know who you are and what the library has to offer. Keep the names and telephone numbers of those contacts in your address file.

Develop programs for all segments of your library's community. Have programs geared to children, young adults, adults, senior citizens, and homeschoolers. Some groups may have a higher attendance rate than others but that is normal.

Develop business partners. Grocery stores and restaurants often donate food to nonprofit organizations. If you are having a special program and would like to serve light refreshments or give away candy to children, call your local grocery store several weeks in advance and ask to speak to the manager. Tell him or her who you are and what you are planning. Most are happy to donate whatever you need. Announce at your program the name of the store that donated the refreshments. After the program is over be sure to send a thank-you letter to the manager on the library's letterhead.

Partnerships with Organizations

There are many organizations in the community that would be interested in developing a partnership with your library. Look in the telephone book for agencies that also serve the community. Think of ways you can both benefit each other. Here are some examples:

1. Your local literacy association. Volunteer to serve on the board of directors. Provide space for tutors and students. Encourage students to bring their families to the library.

2. Child welfare agencies, day-care centers, and other social service agencies that serve children. The agencies could distribute bookmarks, free books, and library brochures to parents of small children.

3. Churches and other places of worship. Library program schedules could be given to the secretaries to read to the congregation or place on their bulletin board. You could ask them what books they would like the library to own to help them spread their messages to the community.

4. Schools. You could do storytimes and speak to parents and teachers at Parent Teacher Association meetings. You could also have a library-card registration drive at all schools in your area.

5. Health offices, pediatric departments in particular. Deposit children's books and brochures for parents. Adult bookmarks for specific genres and bookmarks that promote your library's services could be distributed at all health-care facilities.

6. Senior citizen centers. Invite senior centers to bus their residents to the library on a regular basis. Offer large-print books, book talks, and adult programming during their visits.

7. Civic clubs—Kiwanis, Rotary, Lion, and Jaycees, to name a few. Those clubs usually donate money for programs that benefit the community. Offer your meeting rooms for their use.

8. Adults who would like to volunteer their services to the library could pick up and deliver books to agencies.

9. The local shopping malls. Library staff could read stories to children during some of their events. Bookmarks should be available at information booths.

Library Cards for Organizations

Organizations or businesses such as day-care centers and retirement facilities may want to have a library card for their employees to use to borrow books for their readers. It is important for all members of the community to have access to your library. See what the policy is on registering businesses for corporate library cards. Generally, the manager of the facility writes a letter to the library on their letterhead. The letter states the names of the employees who have permission to use the card, the person responsible for paying overdue fees, and whether or not a limit is placed on the number of materials checked out on that card at any one time. The letter should be signed by the manager of the facility and sent to your attention as manager of the branch. The organization is responsible for monitoring the use of the library card and they will have physical possession of it.

Suggestion Box

Solicit feedback from you community. Have a suggestion box somewhere in the library away from the service desk. This allows patrons the privacy to make suggestions without being identified. Take those suggestions, good and bad, and talk to your staff about them. Try to deal effectively with recurring suggestions.

Publicity

Always publicize your programs well ahead of time. This can be accomplished by putting up posters, distributing flyers, word of mouth, newspaper articles, or an activities calendar that displays all programs within the library system. This is essential for attendance at your library's programs. The only exception is if you have a guaranteed audience like an invited school group that is visiting just to attend this special program.

Have a regular article in your community's local newspaper. Highlight the library and include the titles of new books received and any upcoming programs. Invite people to come in and see new displays that may have been put up recently.

News Media

If your library system has a public relations person, make sure you let her know well in advance of any upcoming programs or events that you would like publicized in the news media. Give her the day, date, time, and a detailed description of your program. Let her know whether you want it advertised in the newspaper, on television, or radio. If there is no public relations person, talk to your boss about the library system's policy on contacting the media. If there is a community newspaper that serves your area, contact them. Ask if they would allow you to have a column to announce programming, library news, or new books. They may well allow you to do it free of charge.

Newsletters

Think about developing a newsletter for your branch. If you have publishing software available you can print and distribute library information to the public. Include a calendar with dates displaying library events. Ask staff what they are reading and include that in every issue. Here are some other items you might want to include:

1. New books and materials.

2. Storytime registration dates.

3. Tips for patrons. These tips include such things as "Books can be checked out and returned to any branch."

4. New computer databases.

5. Any holidays occurring that month.

Make your newsletter colorful, neat, and informative.

Flyers

When producing flyers for library-sponsored events, make sure all relevant information is included. Colorful eye-catching paper will draw attention to the flyers. Use computer clip art or digital photographs to enhance the appearance of your flyers. If your library system has a logo, use it on all publicity materials. All flyers, invitations, posters, brochures, etc., should include the following:

1. Title of event.

2. Brief description of the event.

3. When it will take place.

4. Location of the event.

5. Comments—Age group targeted and whether or not registration is required. For example, if you are doing a program on finances and patrons need to preregister, include the line "Please preregister at the Information Desk."

Place flyers on the service desk and include one in each patron's stack of books as they check out.

BULLETIN BOARD

If you have a bulletin board that is in a public area, set up guidelines for its use. If you don't, you will have a board crammed full of papers, business cards, flyers, and pictures. First, decide what you want to have displayed on the bulletin board. Will it be community events only? Library events only? Information submitted by patrons? Make sure your guidelines are clearly posted. Should patrons put information on the bulletin board at will or should all flyers be approved? The following are issues that must be addressed in any bulletin-board guidelines:

1. Type of information displayed. What type of information do you want displayed? Decide what you want to include and only include those items that are in that category.

2. Length of time it will be displayed. Decide what you think is an appropriate length of time to display general flyers. Those with event dates should be removed as soon as the events are over.

3. Size of flyers. Obviously you cannot have a large poster size flyer on your bulletin board. 8½" by 11" or smaller will accommodate more flyers. You

need to have a minimum size so that your bulletin board does not fill up with business cards.

4. Should the manager approve it? You or someone on your staff should approve all submissions by patrons. You don't want to have something posted that is offensive to patrons. Either stamp it or have a staff member sign and date it so you know when it was placed on the board and that it was approved.

5. Will you accept handwritten flyers? Decide whether or not you want to accept handwritten submissions. Make your bulletin board as neat and professional-looking as possible.

6. Who will be responsible for monitoring and removing dated information? Designate a staff member to monitor the bulletin board for expired flyers and those placed without permission.

7. What is the procedure for flyers placed on the bulletin board without approval? If flyers do not meet your guidelines they should be removed immediately. Post your guidelines next to the bulletin board so that patrons know what they are.

Word of Mouth

Many successful programs have been publicized by word of mouth. If you have an upcoming program that might be of interest to patrons using the library, let them know about it. If you are having a children's program soon, when adults come to the service desk with their children to check out books, tell them about the program. You will be surprised at the number of people who do not read signs or flyers.

Community Service Workers

It is almost inevitable that at one time or another patrons will ask to do community service or volunteer work at your branch. There are two types of community service that you will be asked to consider for temporary employment: juveniles who need to perform community service for a class that they are taking at school, or juveniles for whom community service has been ordered by a court.

Students asking to do volunteer work for class usually only need a few hours of work to complete their assignments. If you decide to allow students to work at your branch, make sure you have parental contact information for them in the event of an emergency. Provide a sign-in sheet with their name, time in, work accomplished, and time out. The students usually have a handout from their teacher that you need to sign when they have completed their assigned hours. Duties that you might ask them to do include the following:

1. Stamping date-due cards.

2. Placing returned books in shelf-list order for shelving.

3. Straightening the shelves to look neat.

4. Arranging magazines and newspapers in chronological order by date. (The most recent edition should be first.)

5. Rewinding video tapes.

6. Picking up loose books and magazines from tables and chairs.

I'm sure that you have many duties that the students could help you with. Make up your own list. Display the list where your staff can refer to it when the students come in.

The other type of community service is court ordered. You can make the decision as to whether or not you want to allow these individuals to work at your branch. I personally have used over 100 juveniles and adults in community service at my facilities. I believe in giving people a chance, and if a particular individual does not work out, she can always be discharged from working at your branch. I think overall it is a good program but you must set guidelines. If someone comes in and asks to do community service, I tell them that I have to meet with their court-appointed caseworker. Once I speak with the caseworker, I let the offender know what duties they will be expected to perform. I also get the time log from the caseworker and keep it until the offender has either completed their required hours or been discharged. A member of my staff or I record the hours worked and place our initials next to the time for verification. It seems to work out much better when I deal with the caseworker rather than directly with the offender.

The offenders have committed nonviolent crimes and most of them are good workers who just want to put the incidents behind them. The restitution program usually has insured them so your library should not be liable for any accidents.

The workers perform some of the same duties as the students doing volunteer work for school. In addition to the regular duties, I also ask the court-ordered individuals to do things such as picking up trash on the grounds, taking out the recycling materials and placing them in bins, cleaning the staff refrigerator and helping us to process discards. If I have any problems with their attitude, work performance, or attendance, I call their caseworker and they in turn talk to the offender. If the problem is repeated, I call and ask that they be discharged.

19

Programming

Library programs are among the important services your branch can provide to your patrons and the wider community. Make sure that your programs are free and open to the public. You may have programs that are specifically geared to certain segments of the community but make sure that everyone knows that they are welcome.

Ask patrons what types of programs they would like to see at the library.

Look in the newspaper to see what workshops are offered in the area. Offer programs on similar subjects. Patrons will be more inclined to attend those at your branch because they are free.

Ask community members if they would host free workshops at the library. Make sure that they are professionals in the subject area. For example, a cardiologist could do a workshop on the prevention of heart disease. An attorney could do a workshop on writing a will. Tap into your community and see what a wealth of resources you have available. If the person hosting the workshop must be paid and you really want to have them do a program, ask the Friends of the Library if they would be willing to sponsor the program.

The following are some possible general and special programs that you may want to offer at your branch:

CHILDREN'S PROGRAMMING

Crafts	Dress as your favorite character
Holiday programs	Puppet shows
Safety	Storytimes

YOUNG-ADULT PROGRAMMING

Applying to colleges	Babysitting 101
Beauty tips	Contests—Photography, Talent
Cultural diversity	Exercise and health
Exit exam review	Gangs
GED preparation	Health for teens
How to use the library	Improving study skills

Job applications made easy
Making after-school snacks
Safe body piercing and tattooing
Single parenting for teens

Latchkey safety
Research paper assistance
SAT preparation

ADULT PROGRAMMING

ADHD—the facts
African-American history
Book clubs/talks
Buying a new or used car
Cancer care
Choosing a nursing home
College financial planning
Cosmetic surgery—is it for you?
Credit repair
Discipline without spanking
Financial independence for women
Grief management
Hospice care
How to file for divorce
Investments
Money management
Mutual funds
Parenting your special-needs child
Personal computer/Internet basics
Self defense for women
Starting a new business
Wills and estates
Your 401K
Your IRA

Adults returning to college
Alzheimer's disease for caregivers
Buying a computer
Buying or selling your home
Child care
Classic film series
Controlling your cholesterol
Craft workshops
Defusing stress
English as a second language
Garden care
Health topics
How to file for bankruptcy
Income tax assistance
Library orientation
Motivating your school-aged child
Organizing your personal files
Parenting your teen
Retirement planning
Standardized tests preparation
Weight loss naturally
Yoga for beginners
Your family tree
Your new baby

SENIOR-CITIZEN PROGRAMMING

Armchair traveler
Book talks
Cooking and nutrition
Geriatric health and well-being
Local history
Talking to your doctor

Bingo
Civil rights for the elderly
Exercise
Library services for seniors
Low-cholesterol cooking
Volunteering in your community

Storytimes

One of the most popular—and worthwhile—programs you can offer is regular storytimes for children. When you or your staff plan storytimes, keep in mind the ages of the children and the materials that would be appropriate for them; the younger the child, the shorter the attention span. Plan to read interactive books; do finger plays, flannel-board stories or puppet shows for very young children. Kindergarten children will love stories with lots of pictures. Don't just sit and read to them, however. Learn how to read while holding the book for everyone to see the pictures.

There are many books available to teach you how to do successful storytimes. Many have patterns for flannel-board stories and techniques to make your job easier. Have parents register children in advance so you know how many to expect. If you want to have twelve two-year-olds for storytime, start a waiting list after twelve children have registered. If the number on the waiting list is enough for another session, plan that other session for a different day.

The books that you use for storytime should not be taken from your collection of circulating books. When you receive new children's books, decide which ones you want to use exclusively for storytime. Change the designation in the computer to reflect that those titles are not available for checkout. Order additional copies to circulate. This way you will always have your books readily available when you need to use them and they will be in good condition. The books that you use in storytime will be part of your professional collection. Visit other branches when they have their storytimes. Talk to children's librarians. Get ideas about which titles work and which don't.

Before attempting to do a storytime session, observe someone with more experience. Watch the way he holds the book, how he talks to children, and what books he reads. Look around to see how children are reacting to the story. Are they participating or do they look bored? Read books on performing storytimes for children. Go to workshops. Ask children's librarians from other branches what works for them. Practice at home in front of your own children. If you don't have children, videotape your performance and critique yourself. When considering storytimes for children, keep these things in mind:

1. Make sure the books you read are appropriate titles for the age of the children you are reading to.

2. Smile and greet each child.

3. Have the same opening and closing each time so that the children know when to get ready to listen and when storytime is over.

4. Alternate nursery rhymes, finger plays, flannel-board stories, and books to keep the session interesting.

5. Use interactive books so the children get a chance to participate.

6. Have copies of the books you read available for parents to borrow.

I have found that whether you have several people who read to children at your branch of if you are the only storyteller, it helps to write down your sessions. I record the date, the name of the group or day-care center, titles of books read, attendance, and anything else that I did with them. This helps me to remember what books I have already read to the various groups. If the children did not like a book, I make a note so that I will not read that one again. (I also record holiday programs and adult programming. It helps to keep up with the various programming we offer and it is interesting to go back a few years to see what we did and how the attendance has changed.) At the end of each storytime, give each child a sticker, a bookmark, or some other promotional material.

School Tours

Invite school groups to visit your branch. The children's department usually conducts tours of the children's area for elementary-school–aged children. Plan a morning for them to come when you don't have any other groups scheduled to come and you are not conducting any instructional classes. Don't invite more than one class at a time because you want the group to be small enough that everyone can see and hear what is being said. When your group comes, introduce yourself and have everyone to sit down. Talk to the group about the library, the importance of reading, and how to take care of library books. Read a story or two if appropriate, then begin the tour.

Explain the different designations of books, how to use the computer to find books, and take them over to each area of the children's section and explain what everything is. Allow the students to ask questions if they wish. Allow time for the students to check out books.

The reference department usually conducts tours of the young-adult and adult areas of the library for middle and high school students. You will not need to read any stories to them but you should explain the library's services and policies. Teach the older students how to use the computerized card catalog and any databases that you have. Tell them your Internet policy. Take the students to the reference area and point out books that are frequently used by students. Let the students know that your reference department's staff is there to help them with research papers, homework, and finding books that they want to read for fun. If you have personal computers for word processing, let them know what the policy is for using them. Let them know about any reservations needed, time limits, and versions of software that are installed on your computers.

Library Anniversaries

The anniversary of the opening of your branch should be celebrated every five years if possible. Advertising and promoting programs for your celebration should begin as early as possible. Let your community know how much you appreciate their patronage. Plan programs for adults, young adults, and children. There are so many things you can do to celebrate! Here are some of my own suggestions; you and your staff may think of more.

1. **A carnival for children**. Plan a cakewalk, face painting, food, clowns, and games. I invite the fire department to bring their fire truck for display.

2. **An adult film festival**. Show classic movies and serve popcorn. If you show video recordings don't forget to purchase the rights to show those movies to a group.

3. **A Book and Author luncheon**. Invite local authors to come in and talk about their books. Serve punch and finger sandwiches.

4. **A Young adult talent show**. Invite young adults to perform in specific categories that you determine. Some examples are singing, playing an instrument, and dancing. By setting categories it will make it easier for the judges to choose winners. Also, you won't have someone presenting a talent that is distasteful. Ask for patron volunteers to do the judging.

5. **A Storyteller**. Invite a storyteller to tell stories that the entire family can understand and enjoy.

6. **Speakers**. Invite the mayor or other community leaders to come in and speak. Local celebrities can talk about the importance of reading to children.

These are just a few ideas that may be enjoyed by your patrons. Ask them for ideas. You might be surprised at how enthusiastically patrons want to help the library.

Book Clubs

Book clubs serve many purposes in your library. They are a chance for patrons to discuss the books offered at your library. Book clubs increase your circulation and allow club members a chance to read books that they probably would not have read on their own. Patrons can have their own book club and use your facility to meet, or one of your staff members could conduct the meetings. Talk to other branch managers about what works best for them.

It is a good partnership when patrons conduct their own book club meetings and use your facility and books. Your branch could acquire the books needed and produce flyers advertising the meetings and upcoming titles to be discussed. Patrons agree to conduct their meetings at the branch and to check out the books needed from the library.

It is always a good idea to have ongoing programs at the library for all ages. We have a book club for adults led by a patron and a book club for elementary-school–aged children led by a children's librarian at the branch. Children can read any book they want and come to the meeting to share it.

Planning a Book and Author Event

1. Line up a co-sponsor for the event. A local newspaper, department store or bookstore are good options.

2. Decide on author(s), working with the date of the planned event. Invite local or regional authors when possible. You may also want to take advantage of promotional tours. Be realistic. Don't expect Toni Morrison to speak! Contact authors far in advance through their publishers' publicists. The Literary Marketplace is a good source of information.

3. Invite the co-host to introduce the author. Ask them to share costs with in-kind services, such as printing the program, invitations, and free ads in their publications. Make plans for getting advance and follow-up coverage in the media.

4. Ask local merchants to donate cheese, wine, and goodies for a pre-event reception. Be sure to give credit on the program, in news releases and during introductions.

5. Make a fuss. Authors like to be catered to. Offer to entertain them at cocktails, dinner, a quick tour, etc., if they are interested. Many authors enjoy talking to a writing class if time permits.

6. Make sure you invite the county chair, mayor, chancellor, heads of departments, local council representatives because they are the men and women who make decisions concerning the library. Often this is an appropriate event to honor someone who has made a special contribution to the library.

7. Remember, most authors are there to sell books. Plan in advance to have copies available for sale and autographing. This is very important. Order more than you plan to sell. You can always return them, but authors are upset if books run out. This is also a way to earn 40 percent of the proceeds, if you order yourself instead of through a bookstore.

8. Make sure someone is familiar with the author's work and can talk knowledgeably with him/her about it.

9. Consult the "Friends of Libraries Sourcebook" for detailed program planning outlines to check your final arrangements.

[Friends of Libraries U.S.A. website *www.folusa.org*. Reprinted with permission.]

List of Performers for Programs

If you regularly schedule people to do programs for your branch, keep their names, contact numbers, fees, other branches were they performed, and a description of their services available for future use. Share your list with other branches and ask them to share their contacts with you. Develop a list of performers for the entire library system to share. If you have contacts who have not performed well or cancelled at the last minute, list them in your directory. Add comments about each performer indicating whether they should be used or not. You can even develop a rating scale and use it for each performer. You can save another branch a lot of time and effort by letting them know that they should not call a specific performer. Each year the library system's directory should grow to include more performers.

Larger-scale Programming

There are already several library programs that you can participate in. The American Library Association explains them on the following pages.

Library Card Sign-Up Month

Try some of these suggestions during Library Card Sign-Up month. Your goal is to increase your registered borrowers which in turn will increase your circulation statistics.

- Present a local celebrity with the large replica of a library card at a library card sign-up event for families.

- Personally congratulate kids on getting their first library card by taking a picture of them holding the big library card next to a local celebrity, their mom, dad, etc. Create a central display of photos.

- Ask your mayor or other elected official to proclaim September as National Library Card Sign-up Month and present the official with the card at the proclamation. Invite media to the event.

- Invite well-known people in your community to submit a two-to-three–sentence statement about the value of their library card. Ask them to pose with a photo of the big library card and design a series of ads. Ask the local newspaper to donate ad space throughout the month of September.

- Encourage rival schools to have a month-long contest to see how many new library card applicants each school can sign up. Rotate the replica card on a weekly basis between the two schools depending on the number of students who sign up for a library card. Ask a local business or community service group to provide prizes to the school that "wins."

- Provide classrooms achieving 100 percent card sign-up with an oversized library card that the entire class can sign and display to showcase their efforts.

- Sponsor a "Why I Love My Library Card" contest. Have students write about why they love their library card. Present the winners of the contest with prizes and get their photos taken with the oversized library card. Invite media to cover the event or take photos and distribute to media.

- Team up with school libraries in your community. Display the card in school libraries during back-to-school open houses with representatives from the library there ready with library card applications. This is a good way to target kids and their parents who attend the open houses.

- Have everyone who participates in a Library Card Sign-up event sign his or her name on the card and display it by the circulation desk.

- Host a read-a-thon at your library. Invite well-known people to read aloud continuously for a weekend at your library. Present each with an oversized library card. This is a great opportunity for news coverage and photo opportunities.

- Host a "First Library Card" event for babies. Invite new parents and their babies into the library for a new-parent workshop with representatives from a local hospital or pediatrician's office. Issue library cards to all of the babies, and take a photo of the parents and babies with the oversized card. Send the photos to local newspapers and to parents.

- Display the oversized card outside of your library. Bring the card to any event in which the library participates such as parades, town fairs, lectures, presentations at the YMCA, Rotary, etc.

- Ask local businesses to offer 5 or 10 percent discounts on a customer's bill for the month of September if the customer shows a library card. Provide local businesses with an oversized card to show that they are a sponsor of the program.

- Have local businesses that cater to kids display the oversized card and randomly ask kids if they have a library card. For those that do, provide the storeowner with prizes to give away, like bookmarks or pencils. For those that don't, ask the storeowners to give out a library card application.

National Library Week

First sponsored in 1958, National Library Week is a national observance sponsored by the American Library Association (ALA) and libraries across the country each April. It is a time to celebrate the contributions of our nation's libraries and librarians and to promote library use and support. School, public, academic and special libraries participate. Some examples of recommended ways to celebrate National Library Week include:

- Posting a National Library Week message on your website. Something as simple as "Happy National Library Week" could suffice, or it could be something more elaborate. Whether simple or lively, the message is sure to be noticed by someone.

- Hang posters in the library, but also ask local businesses to display National Library Week posters and give away bookmarks.

- Invite local officials and legislators for a special National Library Week tour or program to highlight the many ways your library serves its constituents.

- Showcase a variety of your best library resources. Many libraries are fortunate enough to have materials that will include something for everyone, regardless of your patron's age, race, socioeconomic status, gender, sexual orientation, religion, culture, or interests.

- Remind new parents that it's never too late to start raising a reader.

Reach out to low-income and at-risk families. Work with housing developments to offer National Library Week parties, door prizes, storytelling, and refreshments in community rooms. Sign up residents for library cards.

BANNED BOOKS WEEK

Banned Books Week: Celebrating the Freedom to Read is observed during the last week of September each year. Observed since 1982, the annual event reminds Americans not to take this precious democratic freedom for granted. Banned Books Week (BBW) celebrates the freedom to choose or the freedom to express one's opinion even if that opinion might be considered unorthodox or unpopular and stresses the importance of ensuring the availability of those unorthodox or unpopular viewpoints to all who wish to read them. After all, intellectual freedom can exist only where these two essential conditions are met.

The following is a list of ideas to consider to celebrate Banned Books Week:

- Organize a reading and discussion series of books that have been banned.

- Co-sponsor an essay contest with the state library association, a local school, or a community group.

- Use bumper stickers. "Book banning burns me up!" is a popular one.

- Wear T-shirts with clever messages. Bookmarks, posters, and other items are available through the ALA Office for Intellectual Freedom.

- Alert the media. Ask the student or community newspaper to devote an issue to Banned Books Week.

- Stage a mock trial or moot court. Put a banned book on trial and have students argue for and against the book. Select a jury that has not read the book. For mock trial materials and technical assistance, contact the Constitutional Rights Foundation (*www.crf-usa.org*); Street Law (*www.streetlaw.org*); and the Center for Civic Education (*www.civiced.org*).

Create a radio spot. Improve the spot with music! Ask the radio station's technician, engineer, or disc jockey to help you select music and dub it into the radio spot.

[*Whole Library Handbook 3*, by George M. Eberhart. Reproduced with permission.]

CHALLENGED BOOKS VERSUS BANNED BOOKS

A challenge is an attempt to remove or restrict materials based upon the objections of a person or group. A banning is the removal of those materials. Challenges do not simply involve a person expressing a point of view; rather, they are an attempt to remove material from the curriculum or library, thereby restricting the access of others. The positive message of Banned Books Week: Free People Read Freely is that due to the commitment of librarians, teachers, parents, students and other concerned citizens, most challenges are unsuccessful and most materials are retained in the school curriculum or library collection.

[American Library Association website *www.ala.org*. Reprinted with permission.]

The 100 Most Frequently Challenged Books of 1990–2000

1. *Scary Stories* (Series) by Alvin Schwartz
2. *Daddy's Roommate* by Michael Willhoite
3. *I Know Why the Caged Bird Sings* by Maya Angelou
4. *The Chocolate War* by Robert Cormier
5. *The Adventures of Huckleberry Finn* by Mark Twain
6. *Of Mice and Men* by John Steinbeck
7. *Harry Potter* (Series) by J.K. Rowling
8. *Forever* by Judy Blume
9. *Bridge to Terabithia* by Katherine Paterson
10. *Alice* (Series) by Phyllis Reynolds Naylor

11. *Heather Has Two Mommies* by Leslea Newman

12. *My Brother Sam Is Dead* by James Lincoln Collier and Christopher Collier

13. *The Catcher in the Rye* by J.D. Salinger

14. *The Giver* by Lois Lowry

15. *It's Perfectly Normal* by Robie Harris

16. *Goosebumps* (Series) by R.L. Stine

17. *A Day No Pigs Would Die* by Robert Newton Peck

18. *The Color Purple* by Alice Walker

19. *Sex* by Madonna

20. *Earth's Children* (Series) by Jean M. Auel

21. *The Great Gilly Hopkins* by Katherine Paterson

22. *A Wrinkle in Time* by Madeleine L'Engle

23. *Go Ask Alice* by Anonymous

24. *Fallen Angels* by Walter Dean Myers

25. *In the Night Kitchen* by Maurice Sendak

26. *The Stupids* (Series) by Harry Allard

27. *The Witches* by Roald Dahl

28. *The New Joy of Gay Sex* by Charles Silverstein

29. *Anastasia Krupnik* (Series) by Lois Lowry

30. *The Goats* by Brock Cole

31. *Kaffir Boy* by Mark Mathabane

32. *Blubber* by Judy Blume

33. *Killing Mr. Griffin* by Lois Duncan

34. *Halloween ABC* by Eve Merriam

35. *We All Fall Down* by Robert Cormier

36. *Final Exit* by Derek Humphry

37. *The Handmaid's Tale* by Margaret Atwood

38. *Julie of the Wolves* by Jean Craighead George

39. *The Bluest Eye* by Toni Morrison

40. *What's Happening to My Body? Book for Girls: A Growing-Up Guide for Parents & Daughters* by Lynda Madaras

41. *To Kill a Mockingbird* by Harper Lee

42. *Beloved* by Toni Morrison

43. *The Outsiders* by S.E. Hinton

44. *The Pigman* by Paul Zindel

45. *Bumps in the Night* by Harry Allard

46. *Deenie* by Judy Blume

47. *Flowers for Algernon* by Daniel Keyes

48. *Annie on My Mind* by Nancy Garden

49. *The Boy Who Lost His Face* by Louis Sachar

50. *Cross Your Fingers, Spit in Your Hat* by Alvin Schwartz

51. *A Light in the Attic* by Shel Silverstein

52. *Brave New World* by Aldous Huxley

53. *Sleeping Beauty Trilogy* by A.N. Roquelaure (Anne Rice)

54. *Asking About Sex and Growing Up* by Joanna Cole

55. *Cujo* by Stephen King

56. *James and the Giant Peach* by Roald Dahl

57. *The Anarchist Cookbook* by William Powell

58. *Boys and Sex* by Wardell Pomeroy

59. *Ordinary People* by Judith Guest

60. *American Psycho* by Bret Easton Ellis

61. *What's Happening to My Body? Book for Boys: A Growing-Up Guide for Parents & Sons* by Lynda Madaras

62. *Are You There, God? It's Me, Margaret* by Judy Blume

63. *Crazy Lady* by Jane Conly

64. *Athletic Shorts* by Chris Crutcher

65. *Fade* by Robert Cormier

66. *Guess What?* By Mem Fox

67. *The House of the Spirits* by Isabel Allende

68. *The Face on the Milk Carton* by Caroline Cooney

69. *Slaughterhouse-Five* by Kurt Vonnegut

70. *Lord of the Flies* by William Golding

71. *Native Son* by Richard Wright

72. *Women on Top: How Real Life Has Changed Women's Fantasies* by Nancy Frida

73. *Curses, Hexes and Spells* by Daniel Cohen

74. *Jack* by A.M. Homes

75. *Bless Me, Ultima* by Rudolfo A. Anaya

76. *Where Did I Come From?* By Peter Mayle

77. *Carrie* by Stephen King
78. *Tiger Eyes* by Judy Blume
79. *On My Honor* by Marion Dane Bauer
80. *Arizona Kid* by Ron Koertge
81. *Family Secrets* by Norma Klein
82. *Mommy Laid An Egg* by Babette Cole
83. *The Dead Zone* by Stephen King
84. *The Adventures of Tom Sawyer* by Mark Twain
85. *Song of Solomon* by Toni Morrison
86. *Always Running* by Luis Rodriguez
87. *Private Parts* by Howard Stern
88. *Where's Waldo* by Martin Hanford
89. *Summer of My German Soldier* by Bette Greene
90. *Little Black Sambo* by Helen Bannerman
91. *Pillars of the Earth* by Ken Follett
92. *Running Loose* by Chris Crutcher
93. *Sex Education* by Jenny Davis
94. *The Drowning of Stephen Jones* by Bette Greene
95. *Girls and Sex* by Wardell Pomeroy
96. *How to Eat Fried Worms* by Thomas Rockwell
97. *View From the Cherry Tree* by Willo Davis Roberts
98. *The Headless Cupid* by Zilpha Keatley Snyder
99. *The Terrorist* by Caroline Cooney
100. *Jump Ship to Freedom* by James Lincoln Collier and Christopher Collier.

[American Library Association website *www.ala.org*. Reprinted with permission.]

Teen Read Week

This national literacy campaign is aimed at kids roughly 12–18 years old, their parents, and other concerned adults. The goals are to motivate kids to read and to remind parents and educators to encourage older as well as younger children to read for enjoyment.

The ALA Young Adult Library Services Association notes that the number of teenagers who can read but choose not to is growing. Kids who don't read lose their reading skills and reading scores drop. Despite those alarming findings, few if any efforts are being made to focus literacy efforts on this critical age group. In 1998, YALSA launched Teen Read Week, an annual event held in October.

- Plan a community-wide celebration of Teen Read Week in cooperation with schools and youth service organizations.

- Sponsor a "Teen Read Contest." Invite students aged 12–17 to submit their ideas for a national advertising campaign to motivate teens to read. Provide local prizes.

- Display posters and bookmarks. They are available in the ALA Graphics Catalog.

- Invite a popular author to speak with teens. Ask the Friends of the Library to underwrite the expenses.

- Hold workshops for parents on "Turning teens into readers" to give them tips and resources they can use at home.

- Ask local radio stations to air a public service announcement you create.

- Gather testimonials and photos of teen readers. Ask their permission to publish them in the community and/or school newspaper.

- Plan a teen reading camp during the summer.

[*Whole Library Handbook 3*, by George M. Eberhart. Reproduced with permission.]

Celebrating Annual African-American Events

African-American History Month is a time for librarians and faculty to focus on various ways to promote the resources and services available to faculty and students in libraries. African-American History Month can also serve as a motivational time to help instill in African-Americans a sense of pride and accomplishment and to inform the community and the public at large of the accomplishments of African-Americans. Some of the ways that libraries can help to promote the availability of this information include:

- Assisting African-Americans who want to study their heritage.

- Assisting patrons from other cultures who want to research topics related to African-American culture.

- Seeking support for special programs on African-American history.

- Identifying ways to better serve African-Americans.

In addition to African-American History Month, other annual African-American events include Kwanzaa (December 20–January 1) and Martin Luther King Jr. Day (third Monday in January).

Libraries play a key role in providing significant information on African-American history and biographical information on noted African-Americans. In the past, African-Americans did not always have access to these collections, but this has changed.

Celebrating annual African-American events is a time to focus on what libraries have available to support African-Americans in their interests and to provide information and resources that they need.

["Celebrating Annual African American Events" by Gerald V. Holmes. *Whole Library Handbook 3*, by George Eberhart. Reproduced with permission.]

Summer Reading Program

When the school year ends for the summer you will need to have definite plans for what the library will do for the neighborhood children. Summertime is usually the busiest time of the year at the library. If your library system participates in the summer reading program, begin early in the year to plan for it.

Visit the local elementary schools and talk about the summer reading program. Have flyers available for each child to take home giving more detail about the program. Ask each school for their summer reading list. If there are not many schools or not many books involved, pull those books and put them in a separate area to make it easier for parents and children to find them. Put a temporary colored dot or sticker on each book's spine to distinguish it from the rest of the collection. (Make sure that you don't use a dot that is specifically used to identify a genre. Make sure that the summer reading list titles have a sticker or colored dot that is unique to them.)

Have a theme and center your programs and displays on that theme. If at all possible, invite people from your community to come to the library to speak to the children on their areas of expertise. For example, you can ask the neighborhood fire department to come and talk about fire safety. They should come in uniform, explain why they wear what they do, and have the fire truck parked outside to show children about the different parts of the truck. Some fire departments even have portable firehouses that they take to sites. Children go inside these firehouses that look like homes on the inside. They are taught what to do in the event of a fire. You can invite policemen to talk about personal safety, invite a dentist to talk about dental care, and if you have the space in your library, have a karate demonstration by a martial arts instructor. Just use your imagination and the yellow pages of your local telephone directory.

Don't just show video recordings or films. You want the children to be able to ask questions and learn something from the experience. This will increase your user visits because many people will come for the first time just to see your program. Videos can be viewed at home. Most people won't make the effort to come to your library if that is all that you have to offer. Show films if you have a craft or some other hands-on activity at the same time. Keep statistics of your programs and notes about each presenter. You can share this information with other branches. Invite different people each year. If you invited the firemen this year, wait a few years before you invite them again. Try to have new and exciting programs each summer.

Incentives

Librarians often disagree about whether or not to offer incentives for children to read during the summer reading program. Some feel that children should read on their own and not read just to get an incentive. Others feel that the goal is to get children reading even if you have to use incentives. Your library system probably already has your summer reading program in place. Whether you use incentives or not, make your young patrons feel great about reading. Invite local celebrities to read to children or have special summer storytimes where children may read aloud if they want to. The most important thing is for your summer reading program to be successful by promoting and satisfying the joy of reading.

20

Outreach

The purpose of outreach is to bring a part of the library to the community. This can be accomplished through storytimes, or talking to groups, or working together with other organizations to promote library services. Some people for one reason or another will never visit the library. The library should serve the entire community, not just your visiting patrons. Reaching out to your community may increase your patronage and your circulation statistics by encouraging nonusers to become users.

The Homebound

Ask the administration if the Friends of the Library or some other volunteer group offer homebound service. Homebound service is the delivery and pick up of library materials to and from patrons who are homebound for an extended period of time. They may be sick, elderly, or disabled. The Friends would volunteer to deliver books chosen by the patrons themselves or by the librarian from the branch where the books will be originating. These patrons usually are not charged late fees since they are not responsible for returning the items. Avid readers that cannot physically visit the library will be very appreciative of this service.

School Visits

The children's librarian or the branch manager should visit schools on a regular basis. Talk to the teachers and develop a relationship with them. Ask the teachers to let you know when special projects are due. Get to know the media specialists of the local schools in your area. Attend PTA meetings and talk to parents about the services that your library has to offer. Let parents know that you will do whatever you can to help parents and students. Have books displayed for students to refer to for their upcoming projects and assignments. Distribute bookmarks and suggested reading lists for students.

Books to Day-care Centers

To increase your circulation statistics you could consider depositing books at day-care centers. Ask the manager of the center if he/she would consider acquiring a library card for their organization. If they have themes periodically, include books from those themes. Check out books to their facility, deliver them, and pick them up before they are due. Many day-care centers will appreciate the library doing this service for them. Discuss with the manager your policies on depositing books at facilities. Encourage the staff at the facility to acquire their own library cards and invite them to use the library to serve the needs of their families.

21

Your Career Plans

If you are not happy with your job, decide what it is that makes you unhappy. Do you enjoy working with the public? Do you enjoy supervising? What about working with children? What is it that you really enjoy doing that could be developed into a career? These are some of the questions that you must ask yourself in order to make the right choice for your next position. If you don't like working with the public every day, try to find a job in the cataloging department or in the administration. Has it been a long time since your last vacation? You may just need some time off. Before resigning, talk to your boss about taking some time off. Depending upon your library system's policy, you may be able to take several weeks off. Take a trip. Relax at home. When you return to work you will feel renewed. If you don't, think of some other careers that you are interested in. Just because you are a librarian doesn't mean that you shouldn't do other things. There is nothing wrong with changing careers. Maybe you enjoy cooking. You could start your own catering business. Do what you love. If you don't, it will reflect on your performance and your attitude. Find something that you really enjoy and that is rewarding for you.

Resignation

If you are not happy with your job, talk to your boss about it and see if there are any problems that can be worked out. If not, let him/her know that you are looking for other employment. Don't announce at an administrative meeting that you are resigning. Don't tell a colleague hoping that they will tell your boss for you. If you are selected to fill a position in another library system, tell your boss in person. After you have spoken to him/her, let your staff know. If you resign with angry words and hard feelings you may regret it later. Leave on a positive note. You might need a reference from this position, especially if you worked for a number of years. Don't allow negative actions on any job stand in the way of what you hope to achieve later. Always be a professional.

Appendix A

The Freedom to Read Statement

The freedom to read is essential to our democracy. It is continuously under attack. Private groups and public authorities in various parts of the country are working to remove or limit access to reading materials, to censor content in schools, to label "controversial" views, to distribute lists of "objectionable" books or authors, and to purge libraries. These actions apparently rise from a view that our national tradition of free expression is no longer valid; that censorship and suppression are needed to avoid the subversion of politics and the corruption of morals. We, as citizens devoted to reading and as librarians and publishers responsible for disseminating ideas, wish to assert the public interest in the preservation of the freedom to read.

Most attempts at suppression rest on a denial of the fundamental premise of democracy: that the ordinary citizen, by exercising critical judgment, will accept the good and reject the bad. The censors, public and private, assume that they should determine what is good and what is bad for their citizens.

We trust Americans to recognize propaganda and misinformation, and to make their own decisions about what they read and believe. We do not believe they need the help of censors to assist them in this task. We do not believe they are prepared to sacrifice their heritage of a free press in order to be "protected" against what others think may be bad for them. We believe they still favor free expression in ideas and expression.

These efforts at suppression are related to a larger pattern of pressures being brought against education, the press, art and images, films, broadcast media, and the Internet. The problem is not only one of actual censorship. The shadow of fear cast by these pressures leads, we suspect, to an even larger voluntary curtailment of expression by those who seek to avoid controversy.

Such pressure toward conformity is perhaps natural to a time of accelerated change. And yet suppression is never more dangerous than in such a time of social tension. Freedom has given the United States the elasticity to endure strain. Freedom keeps open the path of novel and creative solutions, and enables change to come by choice. Every silencing of a heresy, every enforcement of an orthodoxy, diminishes the toughness and resilience of our society and leaves it the less able to deal with controversy and difference.

Now as always in our history, reading is among our greatest freedoms. The freedom to read and write is almost the only means for making generally available ideas or manners of expression that can initially command only a small audience. The written word is the natural medium for the new idea and the untried voice from which come the original contributions to social growth. It is essential to the extended discussion that serious thought requires, and to the accumulation of knowledge and ideas into organized collections.

We believe that free communication is essential to the preservation of a free society and a creative culture. We believe that these pressures toward conformity present the danger of limiting the range and variety of inquiry and expression on which our democracy and our culture depend. We believe that every American community must jealously guard the freedom to publish and to circulate, in order to preserve its own freedom to read. We believe that publishers and librarians have a profound responsibility to give validity to that freedom to read by making it possible for the readers to choose freely from a variety of offerings. The freedom to read is guaranteed by the constitution. Those with faith in free people will stand firm on these constitutional guarantees of essential rights and will exercise the responsibilities that accompany these rights.

We therefore affirm these propositions:

1. *It is in the public interest for publishers and librarians to make available the widest diversity of views and expressions, including those that are unorthodox or unpopular with the majority.*

    Creative thought is by definition new, and what is new is different. The bearer of every new thought is a rebel until that idea is refined and tested. Totalitarian systems attempt to maintain themselves in power by the ruthless suppression of any concept that challenges the established orthodoxy. The power of a democratic system to adapt to change is vastly strengthened by the freedom of its citizens to choose widely from among conflicting opinions offered freely to them. To stifle every nonconformist idea at birth would mark the end of the democratic process. Furthermore, only through the constant activity of weighing and selecting can the democratic mind attain the strength demanded by times like these. We need to know not only what we believe but why we believe it.

2. *Publishers, librarians, and booksellers do not need to endorse every idea or presentation they make available. It would conflict with the public interest for them to establish their own political, moral, or aesthetic views as a standard for determining what should be published or circulated.*

    Publishers and librarians serve the educational process by helping to make available knowledge and ideas required for the growth of the mind and the increase of learning. They do not foster education by imposing as mentors the patterns of their own thought. The people should have the freedom to read and consider a broader range of ideas than those that may be held by any single librarian or publisher or government or church. It is wrong that what one can read should be confined to what another thinks proper.

3. *It is contrary to the public interest for publishers or librarians to bar access to writings on the basis of the personal history or political affiliations of the author.*

No art or literature can flourish if it is to be measured by the political views or private lives of its creators. No society of free people can flourish that draws up lists of writers to whom it will not listen, whatever they may have to say.

4. *There is no place in our society for efforts to coerce the taste of others, to confine adults to the reading matter deemed suitable for adolescents, or to inhibit the efforts of writers to achieve artistic expression.*

To some, much of modern expression is shocking. But is not much of life itself shocking? We cut off literature at the source if we prevent writers from dealing with the stuff of life. Parents and teachers have a responsibility to prepare the young to meet the diversity of experiences in life to which they will be exposed, as they have a responsibility to help them learn to think critically for themselves. These are affirmative responsibilities, not to be discharged simply by preventing them from reading works for which they are not yet prepared. In these matters values differ, and values cannot be legislated; nor can machinery be devised that will suit the demands of one group without limiting the freedom of others.

5. *It is not in the public interest to force a reader to accept with any expression the prejudgment of a label characterizing it or its author as subversive or dangerous.*

The ideal of labeling presupposes the existence of individuals or groups with wisdom to determine by authority what is good or bad for the citizen. It presupposes that individuals must be directed in making up their minds about the ideas they examine. But Americans do not need others to do their thinking for them.

6. *It is the responsibility of publishers and librarians, as guardians of the people's freedom to read, to contest encroachments upon that freedom by individuals or groups seeking to impose their own standards or tastes upon the community at large.*

It is inevitable in the give and take of the democratic process that the political, the moral, or the aesthetic concepts of an individual or group will occasionally collide with those of another individual or group. In a free society individuals are free to determine for themselves what they wish to read, and each group is free to determine what it will recommend to its freely associated members. But no group has the right to take the law into its own hands, and to impose its own concept of politics or morality upon other members of a democratic society. Freedom is no freedom if it is accorded only to the accepted and the inoffensive.

7. *It is the responsibility of publishers and librarians to give full meaning to the freedom to read by providing books that enrich the quality and diversity of thought and expression. By the exercise of this affirmative responsibility, they can demonstrate that the answer to a "bad" book is a good one, the answer to a "bad" idea is a good one.*

The freedom to read is of little consequence when the reader cannot obtain matter fit for that reader's purpose. What is needed is not only the absence of restraint, but the positive provision of opportunity for the people to read the best that has been thought and said. Books are the major channel by which the intellectual inheritance is handed down, and the principal means of its testing and growth. The defense of the freedom to read requires of all publishers and librarians the utmost of their faculties, and deserves of all citizens the fullest of their support.

We state these propositions neither lightly nor as easy generalizations. We here stake out a lofty claim for the value of the written word. We do so because we believe that it is possessed of enormous variety and usefulness, worthy of cherishing and keeping free. We realize that the application of these propositions may mean the dissemination of ideas and manners of expression that are repugnant to many persons. We do not state these propositions in the comfortable belief that what people read is unimportant. We believe rather that what people read is deeply important; that ideas can be dangerous; but that the suppression of ideas is fatal to a democratic society. Freedom itself is a dangerous way of life, but it is ours.

This statement was originally issued in May of 1953 by the Westchester Conference of the American Library Association and the American Book Publishers Council, which in 1970 consolidated with the American Educational Publishers Institute to become the Association of American Publishers (AAP).

Adopted June 25, 1953; revised January 28, 1972, January 16, 1991, July 12, 2000, by the ALA Council and the AAP Freedom to Read Committee.

[*Whole Library Handbook 2*, by George Eberhart. Reproduced with permission.]

Appendix B

The Family and Medical Leave Act of 1993

The U.S. Department of Labor's Employment Standards Administration, Wage and Hour Division administers and enforces the Family and Medical Leave Act (FMLA) for all private, state and local government employees, and some federal employees. Most federal and certain congressional employees are also covered by the law and are subject to the jurisdiction of the U.S. Office of Personnel Management or the Congress.

FMLA became effective on August 5, 1993, for most employers. If a collective bargaining agreement (CBA) was in effect on that date, FMLA became effective on the expiration date of the CBA or February 5, 1994, whichever was earlier. FMLA entitles eligible employees to take up to 12 weeks of unpaid, job-protected leave in a 12-month period for specified family and medical reasons. The employer may elect to use the calendar year, a fixed 12-month leave or fiscal year, or a 12-month period prior to or after the commencement of leave as the 12-month period.

The law contains provisions on employer coverage; employee eligibility for the law's benefits; entitlement to leave, maintenance of health benefits during leave, and job restoration after leave; notice and certification of the need for FMLA leave; and, protection for employees who request or take FMLA leave. The law also requires employers to keep certain records.

[U.S. Department of Labor website www.dol.gov/esa.]

Appendix C

Explaining Electronic Information Resources to Users

These guidelines are intended to assist information services librarians who provide and publicize new electronic information resources to users and potential users. For purposes of this document, electronic information resources include but are not limited to online search services, compact disc search services, Internet sites, world wide web products, online public access catalogs/systems, electronic texts, multimedia, and other sources of information that users may directly access in an electronic format.

This document offers practical guidance to library staff who are concerned with strategies for implementation, policy, procedure, education, or direct provision of electronic information resources. Though intended for all types of libraries, not every statement will apply to a particular library or type of library. Accordingly, this checklist contains suggestions and recommendations that may be adapted to local library environments.

Planning, Policy, and Procedure

After selection of a new electronic resource, the library staff should determine a schedule for provision of the resource for the users. Planning for this schedule should take into consideration every aspect of these guidelines and may include a time period during which the service is available in a testing/orientation mode for library staff who will be involved in the direct provision of service.

The library should determine which staff will be involved and what their specific responsibilities and assignments will be in the implementation of the electronic resource.

The library should examine existing procedures and policies to determine whether they apply to the new service and, if necessary, develop new policies and procedures.

For electronic-resources licensing agreements or specific restrictions on use, the library should determine which staff have oversight responsibility for observance of any limitations on use.

Information service providers should also conduct planning for staff education, user education, publicity, and evaluation and assessment of the service.

Staff Education

The level of proficiency in the use of the new electronic information resource should be established for each information service provider, including full-time and part-time staff, involved in assisting users with the service.

Some staff may be designated as specialists who will acquire an in-depth knowledge of the service. Others may be designated as generalists who will need a basic or adequate familiarity with the service. A timetable for achieving the required level of competence should also be established.

Staff orientation and training for the new service should include accommodation for various learning styles and may involve a combination of hands-on practice, system tutorials, peer instruction, outside trainers, and/or study of appropriate manuals or other documentation.

User Education/Instruction

Library staff should determine the level of need for formal and informal user instruction for a new electronic information resource.

Library staff should also determine the extent to which the service should be incorporated into existing user instruction sessions and programs and the extent to which new instructional sessions or methods would be helpful.

Planning for user instruction should accommodate various learning styles and may include a combination of point-of-use instruction for individuals, group instruction, peer assistance, system tutorials, documentation, and/or signage.

In whatever form it takes, user education should include provisions for assessment and evaluation.

Publicity

Responsibility for publicity should be clearly assigned.

All library staff who interact with users should be fully briefed and informed about publicity efforts prior to the implementation of those efforts.

Publicity may take a variety of forms, including but not limited to press releases, signage, announcements/letters to the potential user community, special events, exhibits, and presentations.

Assessment and Evaluation

Responsibility for assessment and evaluation should be clearly assigned.

The library should conduct an initial evaluation and subsequent regular evaluations to determine the effectiveness of the electronic resource in meeting information needs of the user community.

Adjustments in the provision of service for an electronic resource should be based on sound evaluation and assessment techniques, including but not limited to the collection of statistical data and surveys of user/staff satisfaction with the resource.

[*Whole Library Handbook 2*, by George Eberhart. Reproduced with permission.]

Appendix D

The Freedom to View Statement

The Freedom to View, along with the freedom to speak, to hear, and to read, is protected by the First Amendment to the Constitution of the United States. In a free society, there is no place for censorship of any medium of expression. Therefore these principles are affirmed:

1. To provide the broadest access to film, video, and other audiovisual materials because they are a means for the communication of ideas. Liberty of circulation is essential to insure the constitutional guarantees of freedom of expression.

2. To protect the confidentiality of all individuals and institutions using film, video, and other audiovisual materials.

3. To provide film, video, and other audiovisual materials which represent a diversity of views and expression. Selection of a work does not constitute or imply agreement with or approval of the content.

4. To provide a diversity of viewpoints without the constraint of labeling or prejudging film, video, or other audiovisual materials on the basis of the moral, religious, or political beliefs of the producer or filmmaker or on the basis of controversial content.

5. To contest vigorously, by all lawful means, every encroachment upon the public's freedom to view.

This statement was originally drafted by the Freedom to View Committee of the American Film and Video Association (formerly the Educational Film Library Association) and was adopted by the AFVA Board of Directors in February 1979. This statement was updated and approved by the AFVA Board of Directors in 1989.
Endorsed by the ALA Council January 10, 1990.
[American Library Association website www.ala.org. Reprinted with permission.]

Appendix E

American Library Association Preservation Policy

Revised 2001

Preamble

The American Library Association's policy on preservation is based on its goal of ensuring that every person has access to information at the time needed and in a useable format. ALA affirms that the preservation of library resources protects the public's right to the free flow of information as embodied in the First Amendment to the Constitution and the Library Bill of Rights.

The Association supports the preservation of information published in all media and formats. The Association affirms that the preservation of information resources is central to libraries and librarianship.

Librarians must be committed to preserving their collections through appropriate and non-damaging storage, remedial treatment of damaged and fragile items, preservation of materials in their original format when possible, replacement or reformatting of deteriorated materials, appropriate security measures, and life-cycle management of digital publications to assure their usefulness for future generations. Preservation issues should be addressed while planning for new construction or the renovation of existing buildings.

Librarians who create, maintain, and share bibliographic records and other metadata associated with physical and digital objects in their collections enhance security, access, and preservation and facilitate collaborative efforts to protect the Nation's cultural heritage.

Librarians must educate the public about the choices and the financial commitments necessary to preserve our society's cultural and social records.

National Information Services and Responsibilities Standards

The Association and its Divisions will work closely with standards-setting organizations to identify and develop standards relevant to the preservation of library collections, participate in their periodic review and updating, identify and develop new standards when needed, and promote compliance with existing standards.

The Association will actively support its Divisions and other organizations in developing preservation guidelines that may serve as catalysts for official national and international standards.

Usability, Longevity, and Durability of Library Collection Media

Manufacturers, publishers, distributors and purchasers of information products must work in tandem to improve the usability, durability, and longevity of the media (e.g., paper, film, magnetic tape, optical disk) that ensure the persistence of these products.

It is the Association's official position that publishers and manufacturers have an obligation and a responsibility to libraries and to the public to report appropriate information about the usability, durability and longevity of media. The Association urges publishers to use paper and other media that meet standards promulgated by the American National Standards Institute (ANSI) and the International Standards Organization (ISO) for all publications of enduring value. Publishers should include a statement of compliance on the verso of the title page of a book or the masthead or copyright area of a periodical, and in catalogs, advertising, and bibliographic references.

The Association will engage in active education and public relations efforts to develop, promote, and publicize standards for the usability, longevity, and durability of information media.

Preservation of Digital Information

Publishers and distributors of content in digital form must address the usability and longevity of their electronic works. The Association encourages publishers to provide to libraries metadata that will facilitate the life-cycle management of works in digital formats and to deposit digital works in repositories that provide for the long-term persistence and usability of digital content. The Association will work with the publishers of content in digital form to develop guidelines on the preservation of digital information to help ensure that such information will not be lost when publishers can no longer retain and disseminate it.

The Association encourages research on metadata, software, operating systems, and life-cycle management techniques that may effect the preservation of digital works.

Public Education on Preservation of Primary Source Documents

Primary source documents from individuals, local governments, and private and public organizations are the fundamental evidence of cultural and social life. Although citizens may sense the instability of newsprint, for example, they may be less likely to know that media such as color film and videotape pose significant preservation challenges. The preservation of primary source documents, if not pursued aggressively, has enormous consequences on our right to know about and understand ourselves and the community in which we live. Libraries have an obligation (a) to inform donors, users, administrators, and local officials about the ephemeral nature of primary source materials, (b) to promote strategies for the proper care, handling, and storage of these materials, and (c) to recommend the use of durable media and methods of documentation.

The Association will help libraries stimulate public interest in this issue and will make information available regarding how concerned individuals, organizations, and governments may act on behalf of preservation.

Federal Legislative Policy

The federal government must provide leadership in developing an expansive and inclusive national preservation policy. This policy should reinforce the mutual efforts of national, state, and local libraries to preserve materials that document our cultural heritage and make them widely available to all citizens. The federal government, by example, by policy, and by the efforts of its historical, cultural, and information institutions, should affirm the responsibility of all cultural institutions, including local and state libraries, to preserve and provide access to historical documents. The federal government should provide incentives that encourage private institutions to participate in the national preservation effort.

The Association urges the federal government to take responsibility for the longevity of information that it publishes on paper, in microform, and in digital formats.

The Association, through its ALA Washington Office and its Legislation Agenda, will strongly support the efforts of librarians to increase federal government funding for preservation programs.

[American Library Association website www.ala.org. Reprinted with permission.]

Appendix F

The Library Bill of Rights

The American Library Association affirms that all libraries are forums for information and ideas, and that the following basic policies should guide their services.

I. Books and other library resources should be provided for the interest, information, and enlightenment of all people of the community the library serves. Materials should not be excluded because of the origin, background, or views of those contributing to their creation.

II. Libraries should provide materials and information presenting all points of view on current and historical issues. Materials should not be proscribed or removed because of partisan or doctrinal disapproval.

III. Libraries should challenge censorship in the fulfillment of their responsibility to provide information and enlightenment.

IV. Libraries should cooperate with all persons and groups concerned with resisting abridgment of free expression and free access to ideas.

V. A person's right to use a library should not be denied or abridged because of origin, age, background, or views.

VI. Libraries which make exhibit spaces and meeting rooms available to the public they serve should make such facilities available on an equitable basis, regardless of the beliefs or affiliations of individuals or groups requesting their use.

Adopted June 18, 1948, by the ALA Council amended February 2, 1961, and January 23, 1980, inclusion of "age" reaffirmed January 23, 1996.
[*Whole Library Handbook 2*, by George Eberhart. Reproduced with permission.]

Appendix G

Guidelines for Information Services

Introduction

Libraries have an inherent obligation to provide information services to support the educational, recreational, personal and economic endeavors of the members of their respective communities, as appropriate to the libraries' individual missions. Information services in libraries take a variety of forms including direct personal assistance, directories, signs, exchange of information culled from a reference source, reader's advisory service, dissemination of information in anticipation of user needs or interests, and access to electronic information. A library, because it possesses and organizes for use its community's concentration of information resources, must develop information services appropriate to its community and in keeping with the American Library Association's Library Bill of Rights. These services should take into account the information-seeking behaviors, the information needs, and the service expectations of the members of that community. Provision of information in the manner most useful to its clients is the ultimate test of all a library does. In that spirit, these guidelines are directed to all who share responsibility for providing information services, including trustees, administrators, educators, supervisors, department heads, and information staff in all types of libraries.

By intent and by design, the guidelines below form a statement of service goals rather than a codification of practices. The reasons for casting these guidelines as goals are two: first, so that this statement can enjoy a long life of usefulness to the profession and to those who libraries serve, and second, to suggest goals to managers and providers of information services. Because these guidelines must serve the needs of all types of libraries, it is recognized that not every statement in the guidelines will apply to a particular library or type of library. Therefore, in applying the guidelines, library staff will need to emphasize those statements appropriate to their particular library, its mission and the community it serves, and they should strive to realize the goals expressed in those statements.

These guidelines address information services from the following perspectives:

1. Services   3. Access   5. Evaluation
2. Resources   4. Personnel   6. Ethics

1.0 Services

1.1 The goal of information services is to provide the information sought by the user. Information service should anticipate as well as meet user needs. It should encourage user awareness of the potential of information resources to fulfill individual information needs.

1.2 The library should develop information, reference, and directional services consistent with the goals of the institution or community it serves.

1.3 The library should strive to provide users with complete, accurate answers to information queries regardless of the complexity of those queries.

1.4 The library should make available user aids in appropriate formats to help users identify items in the collection relevant to their interests and needs. Access guides can list hours, services, floor plans, and other pertinent data about the individual building(s). Guides can also offer assistance in using particular resources or in performing research in a specific subject area.

1.5 The library should provide instruction in the effective use of its resources. Such instruction, for example, can include the individual explanation of information resources or the creation of guides in appropriate formats, formal assistance through tours and presentations designed to provide guidance, and direction in the pursuit of information.

1.6 The library should actively publicize the scope, nature, and availability of the information services it offers. It should employ those media most effective in reaching its entire clientele or selected segments of that clientele, as appropriate.

1.7 The library should survey and assess the information needs of its community and create local information products to fulfill those needs not met by existing materials.

1.8 The library should serve its community by collecting and creating information and referral files to provide access to the services and resources of local, regional and state organizations.

1.9 Based on its clients' known needs and interests, the library should provide information even if it has not been explicitly requested.

1.10 When information is not immediately useful as presented in its source, the library should add value to that information. This process of adding value can range from simply sorting and packaging the information to reviewing and analyzing it for library clients as appropriate.

1.11 The library should participate in consortia and networks to obtain access to information sources and services it cannot provide on its own.

1.12 When the library is not able to provide a user with needed information, it should refer either the user or the user's question to some other agency, an expert or other library that can provide the needed information. Before referring a user to an agency, expert or other library, information services personnel should confirm that the agency, expert or library to which the user is being referred can provide the information and will extend its services to that user. When a question is referred to another agency, the referring library should follow all local, state, regional, or national protocols in effect, including those governing selection of transmittal forms and communications media.

1.13 The library should use or provide access to the information systems outside the library when these systems meet information needs more effectively and efficiently than internal resources can.

1.14 The library should develop and make available to the public a statement that describes the information services it strives to offer all members of its community.

1.15 The library should develop and make available to the public a statement of its reference service policy.

2.0 Resources

2.1 The library should collect or provide access to information resources germane to its mission and reflecting the full spectrum of the population it serves.

2.2 The library should develop an information resources collection and development policy consistent with the goals of its institution or community. These information resources should satisfy through content, currency, format, organization, and quantity a diversity of user needs.

2.3 As necessary, information services personnel should reach beyond in-house collections and in-house expertise by drawing on the resources of other organizations that collect and provide information, by consulting individual experts, and by tapping external information sources regardless of their medium.

2.4 The library should provide access to the most current reference sources available in order to assure the accuracy of information.

3.0 *Access*

3.1 The library should arrange information services according to a coherent plan, taking into account ready accessibility to users. The information services workspace should be large enough to accommodate staff, the collection of information resources, equipment necessary for accessing all communications and other equipment, and users seeking their services.

3.2 The library should make service areas for information services highly visible and accommodate the needs of users, including users with disabilities. Signage should unambiguously direct users to areas where they can obtain assistance in finding the information they seek.

3.3 The library should support state-of-the-art communications methods for access to information resources for all its users.

3.4 The library should provide appropriate equipment in adequate quantities and in good working order for the convenient, efficient consultation of local and remote information resources by staff and the public. This includes communications hardware and software to receive and answer queries for information from users.

3.5 Operation hours for information services should be responsive to the community's needs and behavior and the library's financial and personnel resources.

4.0 *Personnel*

4.1 The library should make available sufficient qualified personnel during the hours that best meet the information needs and expectations of the community.

4.2 Information services staff should endeavor to communicate effectively with the full range of the library's clientele regardless of a user's age, gender, sexual preference, ethnicity, disability, or language proficiency.

4.3 Information services staff must have knowledge and preparation appropriate to meet the information needs of the clientele the library serves. Personnel responsible for information technology services should be familiar and competent in using information technology and should also possess effective interpersonal communications skills.

4.4 Continuing education of information service personnel is basic to professional growth. It is the responsibility of the individual staff member to seek continuing education and of the employing institution to support its staff's continuing education efforts. If possible, the institution should provide continuing education programs.

5.0 Evaluation

5.1 The library should regularly evaluate its information services to ensure that the service furthers the institution's goals and that the goals reflect the needs and interests of the community served. Formal and informal evaluations should be used to determine the optimum allocation of resources to provide quality service.

5.2 The library should integrate the perspectives of staff and community in the overall evaluation procedure for information service.

5.3 In its evaluation of information services, the library should emphasize those factors most important to the community using those services. Among these are response time; accessibility of services (in terms of physical access, convenience of location, convenience of service hours); the value and effectiveness of services for various groups among the population served; and effectiveness in anticipating its community needs.

5.4 The library should gather relevant statistics for use in evaluation. The library should conduct evaluative studies using techniques and measures that will yield data comparable to those from similar institutions and addressing such national norms or common standards as may exist, modified, if necessary, by local needs.

5.5 The library should evaluate individual resources within the collection based upon professional standards and users' needs. It should also evaluate its information resources as a unified information system, including in-house print and non-print as well as accessible external resources.

5.6 The library should appraise the performance of individual information service staff members and of the collective performance of that staff at regular intervals, using recognized personnel evaluation techniques and instruments agreed to in advance by those to be evaluated and those performing the evaluation.

6.0 Ethics

6.1 The American Library Association's Code of Ethics (as stated in the ALA Policy Manual in the ALA Handbook of Organization) governs the conduct of all staff members providing information service.

[American Library Association website www.ala.org. Reprinted with permission.]

Appendix H

Code of Ethics of the American Library Association

As members of the American Library Association, we recognize the importance of codifying and making known to the profession and to the general public the ethical principles that guide the work of librarians, other professionals providing information services, library trustees and library staffs.

Ethical dilemmas occur when values are in conflict. The American Library Association Code of Ethics states the values to which we are committed, and embodies the ethical responsibilities of the profession in this changing information environment.

We significantly influence or control the selection, organization, preservation, and dissemination of information. In a political system grounded in an informed citizenry, we are members of a profession explicitly committed to intellectual freedom and the freedom of access to information. We have a special obligation to ensure the free flow of information and ideas to present and future generations.

The principles of this Code are expressed in broad statements to guide ethical decision making. These statements provide a framework; they cannot and do not dictate conduct to cover particular situations.

I. We provide the highest level of service to all library users through appropriate and usefully organized resources; equitable service policies; equitable access; and accurate, unbiased, and courteous responses to all requests.

II. We uphold the principles of intellectual freedom and resist all efforts to censor library resources.

III. We protect each library user's right to privacy and confidentiality with respect to information sought or received and resources consulted, borrowed, acquired or transmitted.

IV. We recognize and respect intellectual property rights.

V. We treat co-workers and other colleagues with respect, fairness and good faith, and advocate conditions of employment that safeguard the rights and welfare of all employees of our institutions.

VI. We do not advance private interests at the expense of library users, colleagues, or our employing institutions.

VII. We distinguish between our personal convictions and professional duties and do not allow our personal beliefs to interfere with fair representation of the aims of our institutions or the provision of access to their information resources.

VIII. We strive for excellence in the profession by maintaining and enhancing our own knowledge and skills, by encouraging the professional development of co-workers, and by fostering the aspirations of potential members of the profession.

Adopted June 28, 1995, by the ALA Council.

[*Intellectual Freedom Manual*, 6th ed. Reproduced with permission].

Appendix I

Guidelines for Medical, Legal, and Business Responses in Information Services

Originally prepared by the Standards and Guidelines Committee, Reference and Adult Services Division, American Library Association, in 1992. Revised and updated by the Business Reference and Services Section, Reference and User Services Association, in 2000 and 2001. Approved by the RUSA Board of Directors, June 2001.

Introduction

This is the second revision of the guidelines developed by members of the American Library Association designed to assist information services staff in meeting user needs and in responding to users requesting medical, legal or business information. In this edition, revisions are focused on three issues: (1) new terminology, specifically the replacement of the term "reference" with the term "information services," "patron" with "user" and "librarian" with "information services staff"; (2) recognition and incorporation of the impacts that rapidly changing technologies have on the delivery of specialized information services and source formats; and (3) change in focus of the original intention of the guideline from one of addressing the needs of non-specialists at general reference desks to one which addresses the needs of both specialists and non-specialists.

Serving as an enhancement to the information included in "Guidelines for Information Services" (2000), the following issues and perspectives specific to medical, legal, and business information service responses are addressed:

1. Role of Information Services Staff
2. Sources
3. Information Service Responses for Off-Site Users
4. Ethics

1.0 Role of Information Services Staff

1.0.1 A library's information services staff must have the knowledge and preparation appropriate to meet the routine legal, medical, or business information needs of their clientele.

1.0.2 Staff members need to keep current in subject areas and refer questions beyond their level of competency.

1.0.3 Libraries should develop written disclaimers stating a policy on providing specialized information services denoting variations in types and levels of service. The level of assistance and interpretation provided to users should reflect differing degrees of subject expertise between specialists and non-specialists.

1.0.4 When asked legal, medical, or business questions, information services staff should make clear their roles as stated in their library's specialized information services policies.

1.0.5 Information services staff members are responsible for providing complete and accurate responses to users' questions when possible and for guiding library users to the most appropriate resources for their information needs.

1.0.6 Staff should provide instruction in the use of the sources, enabling users to pursue information independently and effectively, if so desired.

1.0.7 If a user has trouble understanding a source, an alternative source should be sought for further explanation or for comparison. If no appropriate sources can be located, a referral should be made.

1.0.8 The information service transaction should satisfy the user's need for information, by providing either accurate sources in hand or clear and concise referrals to obtainable sources and/or services located elsewhere.

1.1 Advice

1.1.1 Libraries may advise users regarding the relative merits of sources, regardless of their medium, and make recommendations regarding library materials when appropriate.

1.1.2 Materials recommended should be the most comprehensive and the most current available.

1.2 Confidentiality

1.2.1 Confidentiality of user requests, both in-person and off-site, must be respected at all times.

1.2.2 Questions should not be discussed outside of the library except when seeking assistance with an information query and names should never be mentioned without the user's permission.

1.3 Tact

1.3.1 Information services staff should use discretion during the reference interview. While it is important to conduct a thorough interview, this should be done in such a way as to minimize discomfort to the user.

1.3.2 Staff should try to identify the issue in question without intruding on the user's privacy.

1.3.3 Information services staff should be impartial and nonjudgmental in handling users' queries.

2.0 Sources

2.0.1 Each library should evaluate and acquire appropriate sources in medical, legal, and business subject areas that are current, accurate, and accessible to meet the needs of the community served.

2.0.2 Users have a right to access information available in library collections within the parameters of copyright and licensing agreements. Information should not be withheld from a user unless the use of a resource in providing that information violates a licensing agreement.

2.0.3 Information services staff should direct the user to possible sources where the information the user requires would be provided. These sources may include in-house print and non-print collections as well as access to external resources.

2.0.4 Aids that assist users in identifying, using, and evaluating relevant sources should be made available.

2.1 Currency of Sources

2.1.1 Libraries should provide the most current information possible, consistent with the needs of the library's primary clientele and within the limitations of the library's materials budget and collection development policy.

2.1.2 User guides should be periodically evaluated to remove references to dated materials.

2.1.3 Information services collections should be weeded to withdraw or transfer dated materials to the general collections.

2.1.4 Currency of publication dates should be made clear to the user in the case of information and information resources of a time-sensitive nature.

2.1.5 Since information in medical, legal, and business areas changes rapidly, the user should be advised that there might be more current information available elsewhere on the topic.

2.2 Accuracy of Sources

2.2.1 Information service collections may provide more than one source that answers a user's request for medical, legal, or business information. Whenever possible, information services staff members should assist users in assessing the accuracy of information by providing alternate sources for comparison or explanation.

2.2.2 In cases where advertisements or solicitations may be misinterpreted as information content, staff should assist users in making the differentiation whenever possible.

2.3 Referrals to Other Sources

2.3.1 Information services staff should make every effort to answer user's questions in accordance with local information services and collection development policies.

2.3.2 If the question cannot be answered using available sources and personnel, they should be prepared to refer questions to individuals as well as to published sources in a variety of formats.

2.3.3 Referrals should be made to other sources only if the agency, service, or individual will extend its services to that user.

2.3.4 Awareness of community, state, and private services outside of the library is important and referrals to services should follow any protocols in effect.

2.3.5 Staff may not make recommendations to specific lawyers, legal firms, doctors, other medical care providers or business professionals but may provide access to other information that may help the user identify and locate those resources.

3.0 Information Service Responses for Off-site Users

Off-site users include both affiliated and non-affiliated users requesting assistance from remote locations.

3.1 Special care must be taken with off-site requests for assistance since it is easy to misinterpret voice messages, and text-based communication may need explanations or interpretation.

3.2 Each library should develop information service policies that include provisions for off-site requests.

3.3 Requestors may have to be informed that the library does have information on the topic but that they will need to come into the library to use in-house print and non-print materials and for further research assistance.

4.0 Ethics

The American Library Association's current Code of Ethics (as stated in the ALA Policy Manual in the ALA Handbook of Organization) governs the conduct of all staff members providing the information service.

[*Whole Library Handbook 2,* by George Eberhart. Reproduced with permission.]

Appendix J

Library Services for the Poor

The American Library Association promotes equal access to information for all persons, and recognizes the urgent need to respond to the increasing number of poor children, adults, and families in America. These people are affected by a combination of limitations, including illiteracy, illness, social isolation, homelessness, hunger, and discrimination, which hamper the effectiveness of traditional library services. Therefore, it is crucial that libraries recognize their role in enabling poor people to participate fully in a democratic society, by utilizing a wide variety of available resources and strategies. Concrete programs of training and development are needed to sensitize and prepare library staff to identify poor people's needs and deliver relevant services. And within the American Library Association the coordinating mechanisms for programs and activities dealing with poor people in various divisions, offices, and units should be strengthened, and support for low-income liaison activities should be enhanced.

Policy Objectives

The American Library Association shall implement these objectives by:

1. Promoting the removal of all barriers to library and information services, particularly fees and overdue charges.

2. Promoting the publication, production, purchase, and ready accessibility of print and nonprint materials that honestly address the issues of poverty and homelessness, that deal with poor people in a respectful way, and that are of practical use to low-income patrons.

3. Promoting full, stable, and ongoing funding for existing legislation programs in support of low-income services, and for proactive library programs that reach beyond traditional service sites to poor children, adults, and families.

4. Promoting training opportunities for librarians, in order to teach effective techniques for generating public funding to upgrade library services to poor people.

5. Promoting the incorporation of low-income programs and services into regular library budgets in all types of libraries, rather than the tendency to support these projects solely with "soft money" like private or federal grants.

6. Promoting equity in funding adequate library services for poor people in terms of materials, facilities, and equipment.

7. Promoting supplemental support for library resources for and about low-income populations by urging local, state, and federal governments, and the private sector, to provide adequate funding.

8. Promoting increased public awareness—through programs, displays, bibliographies, and publicity—of the importance of poverty-related library resources and services in all segments of society.

9. Promoting the determination of output measures through the encouragement of community needs assessments, giving special emphasis to assessing the needs of low-income people and involving both antipoverty advocates and poor people themselves in such assessments.

10. Promoting direct representation of poor people and antipoverty advocates through appointment to local boards and creation of local advisory committees on service to low-income people, such appointments to include library-paid transportation and stipends.

11. Promoting training to sensitize library staff to issues affecting poor people and to attitudinal and other barriers that hinder poor people's use of libraries.

12. Promoting networking and cooperation between libraries and other agencies, organizations, and advocacy groups in order to develop programs and services that effectively reach poor people.

13. Promoting the implementation of an expanded federal low-income housing program, national health insurance, full-employment policy; living minimum wage and welfare payments, affordable day care, and programs likely to reduce, if not eliminate, poverty itself.

14. Promoting among library staff the collection of food and clothing donations, volunteering personal time to antipoverty activities and contributing money to direct-aid organizations.

15. Promoting related efforts concerning minorities and women, since these groups are disproportionately represented among poor people.

[*Whole Library Handbook 2*, by George Eberhart. Reproduced with permission.]

Appendix K

Guidelines for Library Services to Older Adults

1.0 Integrate library service to older adults into the overall library plan, budget and service program.

It is essential for the leaders and policy makers of the library to understand that service for older adults is not a fad; that the need and demand for library services will only increase; that the stereotypical perceptions about older adults and libraries no longer hold; and that nothing short of a total moral and financial commitment to library services for older adults will meet the needs and demands of the present and future older library user.

> 1.1 Acknowledge the changing needs of older adults in the library's strategic planning and evaluation process.
>
> 1.2 Incorporate funding for materials and services for older adults in the library's operating budget.
>
> 1.3 Actively seek supplemental funding for programs and services to older adults

2.0 Provide access to library buildings, materials, programs, and services for older adults.

That older adults may have easy access to library services, library materials, and programs is a primary need. Staff attention to the environmental needs of older adults with visual, physical, and aural acuity deficits benefits more than just seniors. The Americans with Disabilities Act (ADA) of 1990 provides basic guidelines for access to buildings and services for people with disabilities, among which are many older adults. Knowledge of the community, attention to local populations and end-users should further guide library staff and administrators in the provision of appropriate services and programs.

184

2.1 Ensure easy access to library buildings by older adults.

2.2 Provide lighting, signage and furniture that is compatible with older adults' needs.

2.3 Permit older adults to access information through its provision in a variety of materials and formats.

2.4 Promote the purchase and use of assistive technology devices for older adults to easily access library materials and programs.

2.5 Provide service for older adults who are unable to visit the library easily.

3.0 *Treat all older adults with respect at every service point.*

All library users, regardless of age, benefit when staff emphasize customer service in their work with the public. Training opportunities which focus on cultural awareness and an avoidance of aging and cultural stereotypes will enhance staff attitudes and communication skills.

3.1 Promote better working skills and communication with older adults or people of all ages through continuous staff education.

3.2 Integrate library services to older adults with those offered to other user populations.

3.3 Assure that services for older adults embrace cultural diversity and economic differences.

4.0 *Utilize the experience and expertise of older adults.*

Older adults have valuable and long-established connections within the community that can enhance the library's performance, its place in the community, and its ability to offer additional service programs. Proactive recruitment, development and inclusion of older adults bring the intergenerational role of library service full circle.

4.1 Recruit older adults to serve as program resources and volunteers.

4.2 Promote the employment of older adults as professional and support staff members.

4.3 Encourage older adults to serve as liaisons to the community.

4.4 Develop opportunities for intergenerational activities.

5.0 *Provide and promote information and resources on aging.*

Today's library collection extends beyond the traditional print and audio-visual materials to electronic and Internet resources on aging. The library's role extends beyond gathering resources to keeping them current and actively seeking means to publicize and promote them. Library staff and administrators should position the library as a primary access point to information on retirement planning, health issues, second career opportunities, etc., to aid caregivers, family members, professionals and older adults themselves.

5.1 Develop collections to reflect the information needs of older adults.

5.2 Act as a clearinghouse for information and resources on aging for older adults, their families, caregivers, and professionals.

5.3 Incorporate technology resources and access to online and Internet services and information into library collections.

6.0 *Provide library services appropriate to the needs of older adults.*

The explosion of accessible information and of service expectations by the public in recent years has changed the focus of library services and programs. Libraries provide a community setting for older adult programming, enabling older adults to develop new library skills, to remain independent and skillful library users, or to enjoy traditional informational or recreational programs. Library-initiated outreach services (e.g., transportation to the library, home delivery of materials, and remote access to collections) benefit more than just one population and help all users increase or maintain independence in using the library.

6.1 Provide programming to meet the needs and interests of older adults and family members.

6.2 Train older adults to become self-sufficient library users.

6.3 Provide older adults with access to or training in technology.

6.4 Develop programming and services to meet the needs of older adults unable to visit the library.

6.5 Publicize services and programs for older adults.

7.0 *Collaborate with community agencies and groups serving older adults.*

Library programs and services for older adults should not replicate those of other agencies, but can complement and support them. Investigate possible joint programs for older adults. Identify resources the library can provide to assist professionals who work with older adults. Contact local AARP chapters, senior centers, meals on wheels, area agencies on aging and literacy programs. Identify continuing education programs offered by area academic institutions that appeal to older adults. Day-care centers and groups working with children provide opportunities for intergenerational activities. Not only can your library assist these groups but they can help to promote what is available through the library and even tap funding sources not usually open to libraries.

7.1 Identify community organizations and groups of and for older adults.

7.2 Identify roles for library and agency staff in meeting the goals of collaborative organizations.

7.3 Partner with local organizations for library programs and delivery of services.

7.4 Work with existing agencies and educational institutions to promote life-long learning.

[Whole Library Handbook 2, by George Eberhart. Reproduced with permission.]

Appendix L

ALA Policy on Library Services for People with Disabilities

The American Library Association recognizes that people with disabilities are a large neglected minority in the community and are severely underrepresented in the library profession. Disabilities cause many personal challenges. In addition, many people with disabilities face economic inequity, illiteracy, cultural isolation, and discrimination in education, employment and the broad range of societal activities.

Libraries play a catalytic role in the lives of people with disabilities by facilitating their full participation in society. Libraries should use strategies based upon the principles of universal design to ensure that library policy, resources and services meet the needs of all people.

ALA, through its divisions, offices and units and through collaborations with outside associations and agencies is dedicated to eradicating inequities and improving attitudes toward and services and opportunities for people with disabilities.

For the purposes of this policy, "must" means "mandated by law and/or within ALA's control" and "should" means "it is strongly recommended that libraries make every effort to...."

1. The Scope of Disability Law

Providing equitable access for persons with disabilities to library facilities and services is required by Section 504 of the Rehabilitation Act of 1973, applicable state and local statutes and the Americans with Disabilities Act of 1990 (ADA). The ADA is the Civil Rights law affecting more Americans than any other. It was created to eliminate discrimination in many areas, including access to private and public services, employment, transportation and communication. Most libraries are covered by the ADA's Title I (Employment), Title II (Government Programs and Services) and Title III (Public Accommodations). Most libraries are also obligated under

Section 504 and some have responsibilities under Section 508 and other laws as well.

2. Library Services

Libraries must not discriminate against individuals with disabilities and shall ensure that individuals with disabilities have equal access to library resources. To ensure such access, libraries may provide individuals with disabilities with services such as extended loan periods, waived late fines, extended reserve periods, library cards for proxies, books by mail, reference services by fax or e-mail, home delivery service, remote access to the OPAC, remote electronic access to library resources, volunteer readers in the library, volunteer technology assistants in the library, American Sign Language (ASL) interpreter or real-time captioning at library programs, and radio reading services.

Libraries should include persons with disabilities as participants in the planning, implementing, and evaluating of library services, programs, and facilities.

3. Facilities

The ADA requires that both architectural barriers in existing facilities and communication barriers that are structural in nature be removed as long as such removal is "readily achievable" (i.e., easily accomplished and able to be carried out without much difficulty or expense).

The ADA regulations specify the following examples of reasonable structural modifications: accessible parking, clear paths of travel to and throughout the facility, entrances with adequate, clear openings or automatic doors, handrails, ramps and elevators, accessible tables and public service desks, and accessible public conveniences such as restrooms, drinking fountains, public telephones and TTYs. Other reasonable modifications may include visible alarms in rest rooms and general usage areas and signs that have Braille and easily visible character size, font, contrast and finish.

One way to accommodate barriers to communication, as listed in the ADA regulations, is to make print materials available in alternative formats such as large type, audio recording, Braille, and electronic formats. Other reasonable modifications to communications may include providing an interpreter or real-time captioning services for public programs and reference services through TTY or other alternative methods. The ADA requires that modifications to communications must be provided as long as they are "reasonable," do not "fundamentally alter" the nature of the goods or services offered by the library, or result in an "undue burden" on the library.

4. Collections

Library materials must be accessible to all patrons including people with disabilities. Materials must be available to individuals with disabilities in a variety of formats and with accommodations, as long as the modified formats and accommodations are "reasonable," do not "fundamentally alter" the library's services, and do not place an "undue burden" on the library. Examples of accommodations include assistive technology, auxiliary devices and physical assistance.

Within the framework of the library's mission and collection policies, public, school, and academic library collections should include materials with accurate and up-to-date information on the spectrum of disabilities, disability issues, and services for people with disabilities, their families, and other concerned persons. Depending on the community being served, libraries may include related medical, health, and mental health information and information on legal rights, accommodations, and employment opportunities.

5. Assistive Technology

Well-planned technological solutions and access points, based on the concepts of universal design, are essential for effective use of information and other library services by all people. Libraries should work with people with disabilities, agencies, organizations and vendors to integrate assistive technology into their facilities and services to meet the needs of people with a broad range of disabilities, including learning, mobility, sensory and developmental disabilities. Library staff should be aware of how available technologies address disabilities and know how to assist all users with library technology.

6. Employment

ALA must work with employers in the public and private sectors to recruit people with disabilities into the library profession, first into library schools and then into employment at all levels within the profession.

Libraries must provide reasonable accommodations for qualified individuals with disabilities unless the library can show that the accommodations would impose an "undue hardship" on its operations. Libraries must also ensure that their policies and procedures are consistent with the ADA and other laws.

7. Library Education, Training and Professional Development

All graduate programs in library and information studies should require students to learn about accessibility issues, assistive technology, the needs of people with disabilities both as users and employees, and laws applicable to the rights of people with disabilities as they impact library services.

Libraries should provide training opportunities for all library employees and volunteers in order to sensitize them to issues affecting people with disabilities and to teach effective techniques for providing services for users with disabilities and for working with colleagues with disabilities.

8. ALA Conferences

ALA conferences held at facilities that are "public accommodations" (e.g., hotels and convention centers) must be accessible to participants with disabilities.

The association and its staff, members, exhibitors, and hospitality industry agents must consider the needs of conference participants with disabilities in the selection, planning, and layout of all conference facilities, especially meeting rooms and exhibit areas. ALA Conference Services Office and division offices offering conferences must make every effort to provide accessible accommodations as requested by individuals with special needs or alternative accessible arrangements must be made.

Conference programs and meetings focusing on the needs of, services to, or of particular interest to people with disabilities should have priority for central meeting locations in the convention/conference center or official conference hotels.

9. ALA Publications and Communications

All ALA publications, including books, journals, and correspondence, must be available in alternative formats including electronic text. The ALA web site must conform to the currently accepted guidelines for accessibility, such as those issued by the World Wide Web Consortium.

[American Library Association website www.ala.org. Reprinted with permission.]

Appendix M

Confidentiality of Library Records

The members of the American Library Association, recognizing the right to privacy of library users, believe that records held in libraries which connect specific individuals with specific resources, programs, or services, are confidential and not to be used for purposes other than routine record keeping: i.e., to maintain access to resources, to assure that resources are available to users who need them, to arrange facilities, to provide resources for the comfort and safety of patrons, or to accomplish the purposes of the program or service. The library community recognizes that children and youth have the same rights to privacy as adults.

Libraries whose record keeping systems reveal the names of users would be in violation of the confidentiality of library record laws adopted in many states. School library media specialists are advised to seek the advice of counsel if in doubt about whether their record keeping systems violate the specific laws in their states. Efforts must be made within the reasonable constraints of budgets and school management procedures to eliminate such records as soon as reasonably possible.

With or without specific legislation, school library media specialists are urged to respect the rights of children and youth by adhering to the tenets expressed in the Confidentiality of Library Records Interpretation of the Library Bill of Rights and the ALA Code of Ethics.

ALA Policy 52.4 Confidentiality of Library Records

The ethical responsibilities of librarians, as well as statutes in most states and the District of Columbia, protect the privacy of library users. Confidentiality extends to "information sought or received, and materials consulted, borrowed, acquired," and includes database search records, interlibrary loan records, and other personally identifiable uses of library materials, facilities, or services.

The American Library Association recognizes that law enforcement agencies and officers may occasionally believe that library records contain information, which may be helpful to the investigation of criminal activity. If there is a reasonable basis to believe such records are necessary to the progress of an investigation or prosecution, the American judicial system provides a mechanism for seeking release of such confidential records: the issuance of a court order, following a showing of good cause based on specific facts, by a court of competent jurisdiction.

The American Library Association strongly recommends that the responsible officers in each library, cooperative system, and consortium in the United States:

1. Formally adopt a policy, which specifically recognizes its circulation records and other records identifying the names of library users with specific materials to be confidential.

2. Advise all librarians and library employees that such records shall not be made available to any agency of state, federal, or local government except pursuant to such process, order, or subpoena as may be authorized under the authority of, and pursuant to, federal, state, or local law relating to civil, criminal, or administrative discovery procedures or legislative investigatory power.

3. Resist the issuance or enforcement of such process, order, or subpoena until such time as a proper showing of good cause has been made in a court of competent jurisdiction.

(Revised July 1999)
[*Intellectual Freedom Manual*, 6th ed. Reproduced with permission.]

Appendix N

Access to Electronic Information, Services, and Networks: An Interpretation of the Library Bill of Rights

The world is in the midst of an electronic communications revolution. Based on its constitutional, ethical, and historical heritage, American librarianship is uniquely positioned to address the broad range of information issues being raised in this revolution. In particular, librarians address intellectual freedom from a strong ethical base and an abiding commitment to the preservation of the individual's rights.

Freedom of expression is an inalienable human right and the foundation for self-government. Freedom of expression encompasses the freedom of speech and the corollary right to receive information. These rights extend to minors as well as adults. Libraries and librarians exist to facilitate the exercise of these rights by selecting, producing, providing access to, identifying, retrieving, organizing, providing instruction in the use of, and preserving recorded expression regardless of the format or technology.

The American Library Association expresses these basic principles of librarianship in its Code of Ethics and in the Library Bill of Rights and its interpretations. These serve to guide librarians and library governing bodies in addressing issues of intellectual freedom that arise when the library provides access to electronic information, services, and networks.

Issues arising from the still-developing technology of computer-mediated information generation, distribution, and retrieval need to be approached and regularly reviewed from a context of constitutional principles and ALA policies so that fundamental and traditional tenets of librarianship are not swept away.

Electronic information flows across boundaries and barriers despite attempts by individuals, governments, and private entities to channel or control it. Even so, many people, for reasons of technology, infrastructure, or socio-economic status do not have access to electronic information.

In making decisions about how to offer access to electronic information, each library should consider its mission, goals, objectives, cooperative agreements, and the needs of the entire community it serves.

The Rights of Users

All library system and network policies, procedures or regulations relating to electronic resources and services should be scrutinized for potential violation of user rights.

User policies should be developed according to the policies and guidelines established by the American Library Association, including Guidelines for the Development and Implementation of Policies, Regulations, and Procedures Affecting Access to Library Materials, Services and Facilities.

Users should not be restricted or denied access for expressing or receiving constitutionally protected speech. Users' access should not be changed without due process, including, but not limited to, formal notice and a means of appeal.

Although electronic systems may include distinct property rights and security concerns, such elements may not be employed as a subterfuge to deny users' access to information. Users have the right to be free of unreasonable limitations or conditions set by libraries, librarians, system administrators, vendors, network service providers, or others. Contracts, agreements, and licenses entered into by libraries on behalf of their users should not violate this right. Users also have a right to information, training and assistance necessary to operate the hardware and software provided by the library.

Users have both the right of confidentiality and the right of privacy. The library should uphold these rights by policy, procedure, and practice. Users should be advised, however, that because security is technically difficult to achieve, electronic transactions and files could become public. The rights of users who are minors shall in no way be abridged.

Equity of Access

Electronic information, services, and networks provided directly or indirectly by the library should be equally, readily and equitably accessible to all library users. American Library Association policies oppose the charging of user fees for the provision of information services by all libraries and information services that receive their major support from public funds (50.3; 53.1.14; 60.1; 61.1). It should be the goal of all libraries to develop policies concerning access to electronic resources in light of Economic Barriers to Information Access: an Interpretation of the Library Bill of Rights and Guidelines for the Development and Implementation of Policies, Regulations and Procedures Affecting Access to Library Materials, Services and Facilities.

Information Resources and Access

Providing connections to global information, services, and networks is not the same as selecting and purchasing material for a library collection. Determining the accuracy or authenticity of electronic information may present special problems. Some information accessed electronically may not meet a library's selection or collection development policy. It is, therefore, left to each user to determine what is appropriate. Parents and legal guardians who are concerned about their children's use of electronic resources should provide guidance to their own children.

Libraries and librarians should not deny or limit access to information available via electronic resources because of its allegedly controversial content or because of the librarian's personal beliefs or fear of confrontation. Information retrieved or utilized electronically should be considered constitutionally protected unless determined otherwise by a court with appropriate jurisdiction.

Libraries, acting within their mission and objectives, must support access to information on all subjects that serve the needs or interests or each user, regardless of the user's age or the content of the material. Libraries have an obligation to provide access to government information available in electronic format. Libraries and librarians should not deny access to information solely on the grounds that it is perceived to lack value.

In order to prevent the loss of information, and to preserve the cultural record, libraries may need to expand their selection or collection development policies to ensure preservation, in appropriate formats, of information obtained electronically.

Electronic resources provide unprecedented opportunities to expand the scope of information available to users. Libraries and librarians should provide access to information presenting all points of view. The provision of access does not imply sponsorship or endorsement. These principles pertain to electronic resources no less than they do to the more traditional sources of information in libraries.

Adopted by the ALA Council, January 24, 1996.

[*Intellectual Freedom Manual*, 6th Ed. Reproduced with permission.]

Bibliography

In addition to the sources cited with excerpts included in the text of this book, I have referred to or consulted the following sources:

Albright, Mary, and Clay Carr. *101 Biggest Mistakes Managers Make and How to Avoid Them*. Englewood Cliffs, New Jersey: Prentice Hall, 1997.

Alexander, Jane. *The Five Minute Healer: Easy, Natural Ways to Look and Feel Better Fast*. New York: Simon & Schuster, 2000.

American Library Association Office for Intellectual Freedom. *Intellectual Freedom Manual*. Chicago: ALA, 2002.

Blumenfeld, Larry, ed. *Big Book of Relaxation: Simple Techniques to Control the Excess Stress in Your Life*. New York: Relaxation, 1994.

Brostrom, David C. *Guide to Homeschooling for Librarians*. Fort Atkinson, Wisconsin: Highsmith Press, 1995.

Brown, Barbara J. *Programming for Librarians: A How-to-Do-It Manual*. New York: Neal-Schuman, 1992.

Caputo, Janette S. *Stress and Burnout in Library Service*. Arizona: Oryx Press, 1999.

Drucker, Peter F. *Managing for Results: Economic Tasks and Risk-Taking Decisions*. New York: HarperBusiness, 1993.

Eberhart, George, comp. *Whole Library Handbook 2: Current Data, Professional Advice, and Curiosa About Libraries and Library Services*. Chicago: ALA, 1995.

_____. *Whole Library Handbook 3: Current Data, Professional Advice, and Curiosa About Libraries and Library Sciences*. Chicago: ALA, 2000.

Eppler, Mark. *Management Mess-Ups: 57 Pitfalls You Can Avoid (And Stories of Those Who Didn't)*. Franklin Lakes, New Jersey: Career, 1997.

Fuller, George. *First-Time Supervisor's Survival Guide*. Englewood Cliffs, New Jersey: Prentice Hall, 1995.

Giesecke, Joan. *Practical Strategies for Library Managers*. Chicago: ALA, 2001.

Heller, Robert, ed. *Manager's Handbook*. New York: Dorling-Kindersley, 2002

Kahn, Miriam B. *Disaster Response and Planning for Libraries*. Chicago: ALA, 2003.

Katz, Bill, and Linda Sternberg Katz. *Magazines for Libraries*. 12th ed. New York: Bowker, 2003.

Leatz, Christine A. *Career Success/Personal Stress: How to Stay Healthy in a High-Stress Environment*. New York: McGraw-Hill, 1993.

Reed, Sally Gardner. *Small Libraries: A Handbook for Successful Management.* 2nd ed. Jefferson, North Carolina: McFarland, 2002.

Sexual Harassment Prevention Training Manual for Managers and Supervisors: How to Prevent and Resolve Sexual Harassment Complaints in the Workplace. Chicago: CCH Incorporated, 1998.

Slote, Stanley J. *Weeding Library Collections: Library Weeding Methods.* Englewood, Colorado: Libraries Unlimited, 1997.

Trotta, Marcia. *Managing Library Outreach Programs.* New York: Neal-Schuman, 1993.

West Virginia Public Library Working Standards Manual: Guidelines to Excellence. West Virginia Library Association, Public Library Division, 1992.

Index